The Psychology of Persuasion

The
Psychology
of
Persuasion

How to Persuade Others to Your Way of Thinking

KEVIN HOGAN

PELICAN PUBLISHING COMPANY

Gretna 2002

First printing, May 1996
Second printing, September 1998
Third printing, May 2000
Polish edition, July 2000

Spanish edition, December 2000
Japanese edition, November 2001
Fourth printing, May 2002

---

*The word "Pelican" and the depiction of a pelican are trademarks
of Pelican Publishing Company, Inc., and are registered
in the U.S. Patent and Trademark Office.*

Library of Congress Cataloging-in-Publication Data

Hogan, Kevin.
    The psychology of persuasion : how to persuade others to your
way of thinking / Kevin Hogan.
      p.   cm.
    Includes bibliographical references.
    ISBN 1-56554-146-4 (hardcover : alk. paper)
    1. Persuasion (Psychology) 2. Influence (Psychology)
3. Interpersonal communication. 4. Interpersonal relations.
I. Title.
BF637.P4H64 1996
153.8'52—dc20   96-3423
                                                     CIP

Manufactured in the United States of America

Published by Pelican Publishing Company, Inc.
1000 Burmaster Street, Gretna, Louisiana 70053

To Katie and Jessica,
the loves of my life

Contents

Acknowledgments

Thank you to the tens of thousands of children who have listened to me talk to them about the dangers of drugs and alcohol and the benefits of a goal-oriented, positive life-style. Thank you for the lessons in persuasion you have taught me.

Thank you to Harry and Carol Swicker and Dr. Charles Hogan and his beautiful wife, Frances. Thank you for your love.

Thank you to Jessica Lynn Hogan for reminding me about hugs and love.

Thank you to Katie Hogan for giving me Jessica to love. Thank you for typing and editing this labor of love when we could have been doing other things together. Thank you for all your support.

Thank you to Pelican Publishing for having the confidence in this project to make it a reality.

Thank you to the Grand Designer for giving us the great purpose in life, to communicate with each other.

PARADIGM OF PERSUASION

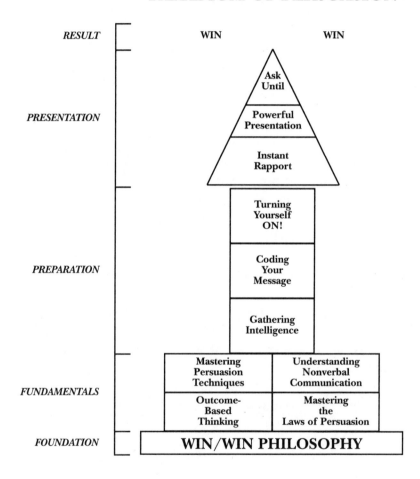

Introduction

There were a dozen or so Twin Cities motivational specialists in the room waiting to meet Dr. Denis Waitley, world-renowned psychologist and speaker. I was pleased to have been asked to join the breakfast meeting with Dr. Waitley. He was prepared to deliver one of his superb talks that evening.

We all sat quietly and listened to Dr. Waitley brief us on his new training system for businesses that would be implemented nationwide. Personally, I was impressed and felt strongly about "The Winner's Edge" program for corporate America.

After Dr. Waitley's briefing, as he sipped an orange juice with his lovely wife who accompanied him, one of the individuals in the room began to downgrade the program in a way that embarrassed the rest of us. Dr. Waitley only smiled and appreciated the gentleman's remarks. As the meeting drew to a close, the same gentleman stood up. Dr. Waitley stood up as well and said, "John, I want to thank you for coming today and giving me your feedback. You're a winner, John."

John smiled, turned, and walked away saying good-bye.

At least three people walked out of the room that morning feeling better about themselves than when they walked in:

1. John, whose self-esteem was boosted.

2. Dr. Waitley, who could be comforted that he showed compassion to a frustrated businessman.
3. Me, who understood another dimension of the term WIN/WIN.

WIN/WIN is not simply a pie-in-the-sky notion. It is a way of life—everyday life. Dr. Waitley had little materially to win by his nurturing attitude toward John. He would never see him again. Dr. Waitley simply was himself, always wanting the other person to win, even when there is nothing material for him to win. The "win" for him is the personal satisfaction that comes from acting fairly. This is what the WIN/WIN philosophy of life is all about. It is a belief and a high value. One of my goals it to help people operate in a WIN/WIN way of thinking.

Today, many people deal with their clients and families in ways that either one or both loses.

The subject of this book is persuasion. Persuasion can be good or bad depending upon who wields the power!

This book will describe the psychology of persuasion. We will consider how persuasion works and, indeed, how to become persuasive. We will consider research from therapists, psychologists, salespeople, motivational specialists, and more.

The purpose of this book is to teach you a skill that can be used in your personal life as well as business life. The ability to communicate persuasively is a critical one to the success of any individual.

One of my hopes for you is that you will learn the skills of the Master Persuader and use them to live a more exciting, powerful, and loving life. It is my deepest desire that after you read this book, you will find the relationships you search for and build your own American dream.

As we examine the persuasion process, you will discover more than just how to get people to do what you want them to do. You will discover how to build relationships and listen to others' needs so you can help people in ways you never imagined possible.

If you are a salesperson, your sales will dramatically increase.

If you are married, your bond will grow deeper.

If you are fearful and tentative, you will learn how to turn fear into power and tentativeness into confidence.

It is important to note that this book contains the most powerful tools, strategies, and technologies of persuasion. The information in this book is used by winning political candidates, multimillion-dollar television ministries, and some of the world's most powerful people. Similarly, the exact same tools, strategies, and technologies are used by the best-run businesses in the world. They are used by people who have the happiest marriages and people who love and excel in their careers. They are used by the world's great teachers.

The only difference is in the question of ethics. Ethics is not a black or white issue. One person's black is another person's grey. One person's grey is another person's white. The power of persuasion is easily abused and easily used to manipulate. It can easily be used to harm and create evil. Similarly, the exact same technology and power can be used to accomplish phenomenal good. It is your responsibility to wield the powers of persuasion in an ethical fashion.

No one can determine for you what is ethical. We will discuss ethics and the process of persuasion in detail later.

It is my greatest wish that you will use the power to influence carefully and wisely. With this understood, we will begin a practical study on how you can implement persuasion strategies in your home life and in your career or business. You will soon realize that the power to influence comes into play hundreds of times each day! May your journey into understanding why we do things and how to get others to do things be a fascinating one!

The
Psychology
of
Persuasion

PART I

Patterns of Persuasion

PARADIGM OF PERSUASION

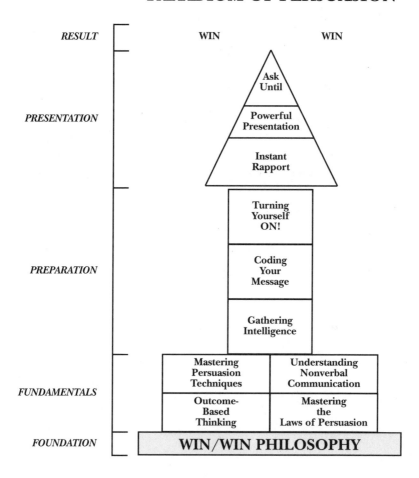

RESULT   WIN   WIN

PRESENTATION
- Ask Until
- Powerful Presentation
- Instant Rapport

PREPARATION
- Turning Yourself ON!
- Coding Your Message
- Gathering Intelligence

FUNDAMENTALS
- Mastering Persuasion Techniques
- Understanding Nonverbal Communication
- Outcome-Based Thinking
- Mastering the Laws of Persuasion

FOUNDATION
WIN/WIN PHILOSOPHY

CHAPTER 1

The Power to Influence

Everyone lives by selling something. —Robert Louis Stevenson

If there is any one secret of success, it lies in the ability to get the other person's point of view and see things from his angle as well as from your own.   —Henry Ford

The ability to deal with people is as purchasable a commodity as sugar or coffee. And I will pay more for that ability, than for any other under the sun.   —John D. Rockefeller

The world would be a very different place without those few individuals who have mastered persuasion skills and used them so effectively throughout the millennia. You may not want to change the world, but with what you learn in this book you will learn the tools and strategies of those who have!

Would you like to be able to have more control over the events in your life? Would you like to be able to state convincingly your side of an issue in a discussion? Would you enjoy being able to persuade your spouse to take you out more often? Doubling your sales is the promise of many seminar speakers. Would you like to know how the true masters of selling produce such astonishing results?

We should define what the psychology of persuasion means and what you can expect to learn from this book.

Persuasion is the ability to induce beliefs and values in other people by influencing their thoughts and actions through specific strategies. Psychology, in its most literal definition, is the study of the soul (the soul meaning the true individual). Therefore, this book is the study of how influence works as a process and how someone can apply the tools and strategies of persuasion to his or her everyday life.

We can understand the entire concept of persuasion better if we remember that we are all motivated toward pleasure and/or away from pain. Whether we are trying to please God or begin a career as a criminal, almost all of our behavior comes down to choosing or responding to various forms of stimulus that take us toward our goals or move us away from our fears. Understanding this simple premise will allow everything in this book to fall correctly into place in your mind.

Simplistic as it may seem, there is something else that will help you understand this book. Each time you come across a term you are not familiar with, consult the glossary in the back of the book, or a dictionary. It is very hard to learn about anything when the definitions of the terms being used are unclear.

The final advice for gaining the most from the book is that you make sure you do the enjoyable exercises provided so you will be able to integrate the information into your subconscious immediately. If you want to be able to persuade others, you really will want to partake in the exercises. If you're just reading to learn how persuasion works and don't intend to use this information, that's another thing altogether! Knowledge is only power when it is applied.

The ability to influence the behavior of another person or group of people has been a necessary element in human culture since the beginning of time. The greatest changes in the course of humanity have all been guided by individuals with mastery in the persuasion process. These people were/are able to convince others that by following their set of beliefs or altering their values, their lives would be better.

There is the well-known story in the Bible of a man who was able to convince a multitude of his fellow slaves to rise up and leave Egypt. The slaves knew, of course, that they could not succeed. It would be impossible to escape from the army of Pharaoh and, once in the desert, there would be no possibility of survival. They had no weapons, little food, and a minimum of possessions. Knowing this, Moses told his people that God had given him instructions to go, spend forty years in the desert, then enter into the Promised Land.

Moses not only had to convince the Hebrews to leave Egypt, he had to convince them that God actually talked to him. Once he convinced the people that God talked to him, he then had to persuade them to believe they would survive the trek to Palestine. What would the fate of the Hebrew people have been had Moses failed to persuade those thousands that he was "for real"? What did Moses possess that other biblical leaders did not? After all, the people listened to Moses. In many other stories, the people all but ignored God's messengers.

Later in the Bible, we learn of a descendant of those very same Hebrews. This man went to all the major cities of the world as he knew it, to tell the story of another man. This man, he said, overcame death because He was the Son of God. Who would believe such a thing? Stories of Messiahs and Saviors were a dime a dozen. What made this persuasive man so effective? Today, upwards of one billion people have been persuaded, through the writings of the Apostle Paul, to believe in the man who overcame death, a man whom he never knew while he lived on Earth! Whether you are a Christian or not is irrelevant in considering the tremendous influence of the onetime persecutor of Jews. In a later chapter, we will discuss in detail just *how* Paul persuaded so many people to *his* way of thinking.

Eighteen hundred years later, a man was heard to say, "If I can persuade, I can move the universe." Unfortunately for this man, his skin was black and he was the property of another man. He wasn't likely to persuade anyone of anything, except that he was worthy of a whipping for his talk of freedom. With few exceptions, no one listened to the rambling of a black man in the mid-1800s. Shortly after escaping to a free land, he became the number-one activist in America. It was his agitation, and doing the impossible, that convinced the white man to support freeing slaves. This powerful man brought the notion to the nineteenth-century political world, and eventually to the pen of Pres. Abraham Lincoln in the Emancipation Proclamation, that all men should be free. The man's name was Frederick Douglass.

Douglass certainly was not the first slave to want his freedom. He was not the first to try to rebel. What was it that made him effective in his pursuit? What skills and qualities did Douglass possess and utilize in improving the prospects for the freedom of all Americans? He was the epitome of what we will call the "Master Persuader" throughout this book. Douglass was a man who could paint a picture in the minds of his listeners. He was able to instill his values in his followers. He was capable of altering the beliefs of his audience. He was unstoppable in his belief in his ambitions and his goals. The "pleasure" of freedom and the "pain" of slavery outweighed the "pain" of recapture and potential persecution once he gained his freedom. Both pleasure and pain, as we can see, can be strong motivators.

The stories of the masters of influence and persuasion are nearly endless. Moses, Lao-Tzu, Buddha, Jesus of Nazareth, Martin Luther, Thomas Jefferson, Benjamin Franklin, Frederick Douglass, Abraham Lincoln, John F. Kennedy, Martin Luther King, Golda Meir, Mother Teresa, Margaret Thatcher, Mary Kay Ash, and numerous others all were people of vision who changed the world. There was more to changing the world than their singular vision of course. It was their ability to influence others to believe in their vision.

The techniques and strategies these great individuals used are the same techniques that salespeople, managers, entrepreneurs, public speakers, religious and political leaders, and activists today need to know to influence others to believe in their ideas.

Consider Anthony Robbins, who wrote the books *Unlimited Power* and *Awaken the Giant Within*. It was his belief in himself and his ability to help others that have helped him create a following of people whose lives have been changed by applying the principles he has synthesized over the years from the great Master Persuaders.

Consider the ability of Bill Clinton to become president of the United States in the face of sexual misconduct, financial improprieties and other scandals. The charges years earlier against Gary Hart were much less than those Clinton faced, but Hart did not possess the ability to influence voters to realign their values and beliefs. Clinton did. The power to influence is certainly the most important communication skill one can have.

You don't need to have the ability of an Anthony Robbins, a Bill Clinton, a JFK, or a Martin Luther King to make an impact in your field or relationships. You do need to understand the skills of the great communicators. Surprisingly, with practice, it is easy to learn them.

There is certainly a very great downside to the power of influence. There will always be the master manipulators. Adolf Hitler, Saddam Hussein, and the like have mastered these influential skills for the worse. It is an unfortunate truth that the skills of persuasion can be acquired by people with both good and evil motivations. The sword of influence can be wielded for the benefit or the destruction of society and for all purposes in between.

Hitler was able to paint a vision of a Germany that would be pure and powerful. He painted as evil those who opposed his positive vision. Millions of people believed in his vision, realigning their values and beliefs with his. However, as happens in the persuasion process, the critical faculties of the masses went unused. The disaster that followed is of course history.

Saddam Hussein, armed to the teeth with weaponry and power, believed that he had the right to "take back" Kuwait as part of Iraq. The masses once again listened, unflinchingly, buying into the picture of the restoration of Kuwait to Iraq.

When President Bush sent the message to Iraq to withdraw or pay the price, Saddam of course did nothing. Saddam's power had been built up in part by the U.S. in the 1980s to set it up as a "balancing power" in the Middle East. Saddam knew that the U.S. might attack but would never destroy him personally as then Iran would be in control of the Middle East. Although he miscalculated on many occasions in the Gulf War, he was correct on the security of his own personal power.

What is clear from these few examples is how values and beliefs play a part in the persuasion process. Your values will determine how you will use your new skills. After reading this book, you will understand the psychology of the persuasion process. You will recognize manipulation as well as ethical persuasion tactics without a second thought. You will be less likely to be taken advantage of. You will become more assertive. You will become happier as you learn that you can control much of your own destiny rather than being a pawn in someone else's chess game.

Today, the power to influence other people and persuade them to your way of thinking is most often the missing ingredient in the success recipe. Many people will set goals, work hard, have high self-esteem, be virtuous in all aspects of the word, yet, they never really achieve their goals, dreams, and aspirations. The reason is that they have not developed their ability to sell their products, services, and/or ideas to others.

Some of the most honest people you know are completely unable to convince others of what they believe. They may be unable to persuade their spouses to eat out tonight! Not only are many people with high integrity inept at persuasion, they often come across as lying and unsure of themselves in the communication process.

There are many keys to success, but the ability to persuade others is the *master key to wealth, love, and happiness.*

In order to influence other people, you need to master persuasive communication skills. Without excellent communication skills, you are highly unlikely to gain valuable promotions, get out of the rut of mediocrity in sales, and have fulfilling relationships. With good communication skills, people will like you, respect you, and do things for you that they would not do for others.

The power to influence is the skill that allows individuals to make quantum leaps on the ladder of life. You can make these leaps as thousands of others have.

Walking is very easy. However, very few infants can walk the length of a room the first time they try. Bicycling is easy. As with walking, children seldom are able to master bicycling on a ten speed the first outing. Mastering persuasion skills is much like walking and riding a bike. It is easy. It takes time, effort, and a great deal of practice. Once you acquire the skills, you will notice they are easy to use and soon will use them without thinking about them. They will become a part of you.

As you learn about the psychology of persuasion, you will gain new insights into how people think, what they want, and how you can help them. Only through helping others can we be truly successful.

Zig Ziglar, the great Master Persuader, often says, "You can get everything you want in life if you'll just help enough other people get what they want." This philosophy is called "The Double Win" by Denis Waitley; Stephen Covey calls it "WIN/WIN or NO DEAL." What you call this philosophy is not as important as implementing it in your life.

This book will often point out how the persuasion process is used by those who do not believe in the WIN/WIN philosophy. These are the manipulators and con men. You need to be wary of them. You need to be able to defend yourself, your family, and your business against their tactics. By learning the techniques of the world's cheaters you will seldom if ever be taken advantage of in the future. Your understanding of the powers of persuasion will act like an X ray to see through rhetoric and determine what someone is really after.

As you turn the pages of this book, you will learn all the elements of persuasion, how to identify them when listening to others, and how to use them in persuading others to your point of view. However, you will not just be given a list of techniques and rules on how to say something to persuade someone. Persuasion is much more than that.

If you were given a hammer and told to go build a house, you would have a *big* problem. You would have no other tools, no blueprint, no lot to build on, no materials, no paint—and you know what? No house would get built!

This book will give you the tools, blueprints, words, pictures, strategies, tactics, and more. You will learn how every movement you make when communicating can affect the persuasion process. You will learn how to use physical space in ways you never thought of before. You will learn about the importance of touching people when trying to influence them. The convictions you hold about your ideas and yourself are critical to the persuasion process and you will see why this is so and what to do to maximize your advantage because of it.

This book will change your life. You will learn how to create positive connections in your life with others. You will determine how to meet the needs of others effectively while meeting your own. Every relationship you are involved in will become more fulfilling as a result of applying the strategies and ideas in this book.

It is important to note that in most chapters you will be asked to recall past experiences in the communication process. Sometimes these requests will be directly stated. As you read about the laws and techniques of persuasion, take each point to heart and truly think about it. Think of at least one time when each law or technique or strategy came into play in your decision-making process. The importance of this cannot be overstated. You will realize quickly how important it is not to just *read* this book. You will see with crystal clarity how this book is a set of tools with instructions and batteries included! The tools are very useful. Many are life changing. The tools need to be used daily and *today* is the day to begin!

In the next several chapters, you will discover the nine laws of persuasion and how they work. You will uncover how the most persuasive people in the world think. The revelations will be exciting and you will probably wonder why you haven't been using this kind of power before! We will discuss how to use these laws of persuasion in our everyday communication. Remember, in each new area under discussion, recall a time when the specific laws, processes, or strategies were used in your communication and the results that followed.

As you read through the pages of this book, think about how the media uses the strategies and techniques every day to get you to purchase their products. How do your church leaders use the strategies? How do salespeople use the laws of persuasion? How do your children use verbal and nonverbal communication to influence you? How does your spouse influence you? How do you influence your spouse? How can you use each of the laws of persuasion to make your life more passionate, more fulfilling, and more in your control?

Living your life day by day, you know that sometimes it seems as if someone else is "driving your bus." This book will teach you how to "drive your bus" and be very, *very* good at it. Read on and see your life change for the better every day that goes by!

You are going to learn the strategies of the Masters to help you bring pleasure to many people. Used properly, understanding the psychology of persuasion will allow you not only to change your life, but impact those you come into contact with on a daily basis.

PARADIGM OF PERSUASION

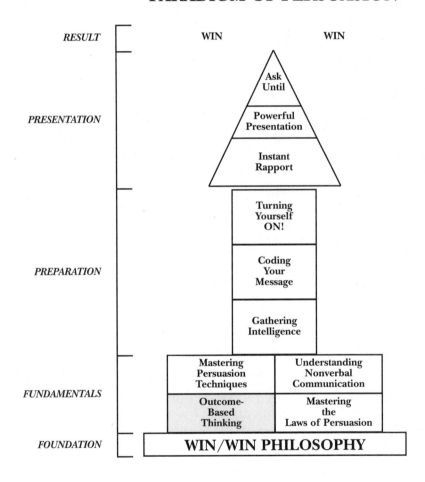

CHAPTER 2

Outcome-Based Thinking

Compared to what we ought to be, we are only half awake.
—Prof. William James, Harvard

The great aim of education is not knowledge, but action.
—Herbert Spencer

Anthony Robbins says that people don't buy products; they buy states. What does he mean?

An individual's state of mind is a very important thing to consider in the persuasion process. It is also *very* important to know the other person's *desired state* of mind. When you determine this, you can persuade the person by showing him how to get there.

In the last few years, exercise equipment has become the latest decoration in millions of homes. Why do people have these often unsightly and bulky machines taking up space in their basements all around the world? Couldn't a person simply go cross-country skiing instead of spending hundreds or even thousands of dollars on simulated ski machines? Why not climb the stairs going down to the basement instead of purchasing stair-climber simulators?

The incentive to purchase these expensive exercise machines is generally first felt when an individual watches the television late at night and sees a 180-pound man in great shape skiing away, making it all look very simple. The message is: Buy the machine and you can look and feel like me. But a lot of selling comes between the initial message and the actual purchase. There are many obstacles to this sale. At the end of the chapter we'll look at exactly how it is done.

While you read this chapter, you will need to have a notebook or about ten sheets of paper and a pen to do the exercises. It is very important that you actually do all of the exercises in this chapter before going on to the next chapter.

Whether you want to become a Master Persuader or simply a better communicator, it is essential to take on the thinking process of a Master Persuader. Even if your purpose for reading this book is simply to improve your relationships or have more sway with those around the house or office, the exercises will be *fun* to do and you will realize after you have done them how important they were!

Most people operate in a stimulus/response mode. Something happens; they respond. Something else happens; they respond. This chapter will show you how to control your world instead of continually reacting to various stimuli. Outcome-Based Thinking will allow you to decide what you want and show you how to get it.

When you go on a vacation, you decide where you are going and how you are going to get there. You also prepare for things that might go wrong. (You make sure the spare has air, bring a gas can and a flashlight, etc.) This is an example of Outcome-Based Thinking!

Knowledge is only potential power. True personal power is the ability to *take action* and *implement your knowledge*. In order to persuade others to your way of thinking, you must become a Master of *Outcome-Based Thinking*.

Outcome-Based Thinking is the ability to visualize the precise

This is a proven system of goal setting that has been used in its exact or similar form by such great leaders as Anthony Robbins, Zig Ziglar, W. Clement Stone, Napoleon Hill, and other people who are focused on what their life is about and know what they want.

Providing yourself with a road map puts direction in your life. Once you know where you're heading, it's much easier to find the way. You cannot persuade others to your way of thinking if you don't know *what* you are thinking and what direction you are going. By giving your life purpose and goals you become a more powerful person. You have *reasons* to be alive and feel fulfilled. These are characteristics people look for when adopting others' beliefs and values. OBT provides you with purposes and goals.

Here is the procedure for using OBT in the persuasion process. Answer each of the following questions. Think of an upcoming event, appointment, or situation where you will hope to persuade someone to your way of thinking. Once you have something specific in mind, complete the simple exercise that follows the questions

1. What precisely do I want out of the process?

2. What does the other person want? If I don't know, what is he likely to want?

3. What is the least I will accept out of the process?

4. What problems could come up in the process?

5. How will I deal with each one and, if possible, use the problem as a *benefit* for the other person?

6. How will I bring the process to a conclusion?

All Master Persuaders use this process, whether they are conscious of it or not.

Imagine that you are a real-estate agent, selling a newly listed house. We will follow your thinking process using the OBT questions.

1. *What precisely do I want out of the process?* You want a maximum commission. Every thousand dollars of house sold is worth $30 in commission to the agent. You want the house to sell at $99,000. You want to sell it today, or at least get a purchase agreement today.

2. *What does the other person want? If I don't know, what is he likely to want?* The client wants to be reassured that he isn't making a mistake. He wants to know he will be happy in the house he purchases. He doesn't want to be pressured. He will want a lower price, probably around $93,000.

3. *What is the least I will accept out of the process?* You will not recommend making an offer for less than $94,900. (Of course, being a representative of the buyer, you must make any offer he wishes!)

4. *What problems could come up in the process?* The client may not qualify for the loan. The most obvious problem is that he will want to think about it for a day, a week, or longer. He might want an independent inspection and that would slow up the process. He might find something wrong with the house.

5. *How will I deal with each one and, if possible, use the problem as a benefit for the other person?* a. If he doesn't get the loan due to bad credit, that is beyond your control. b. If he needs to think about it, you can remind him how quickly the last house he looked at sold. You'll note that fact when he is most excited about buying. c. If he wants an inspector, write up the agreement contingent upon inspector approval. Get it in writing today! d. If he finds something

wrong with the house, you will turn it to his benefit by using it as a bargaining tool with the seller, conceding one or two thousand dollars.

6. *How will I bring the process to a conclusion?* You will conclude the process at the peak of the emotional state, confirm the highest dollar figure to be offered, and stress the urgency involved.

I recently visited our local Toyota dealership to purchase a Camry. Here's how I used this exact process.

1. *What precisely do I want out of the process?* I want to buy a new Toyota Camry with only specific options. I want it for $300 under invoice.

2. *What does the other person want? If I don't know, what is he likely to want?* The salesman needs to sell the car for more than $100 over invoice to earn more than a token commission. One thing is certain. He does want to sell a car. The dealership probably has pressure on salesmen to sell at least ten to fifteen this month for dealer incentives, so any sale is worthwhile for him.

3. *What is the least I will accept out of the process?* I will pay as much as $300 over the *Consumer Reports* invoice data, and not a penny more.

4. *What problems could come up in the process?* I will be kept waiting for hours for approval from the finance manager of my modest offer. They may refuse my offer.

5. *How will I deal with each one and, if possible, use the problem as a benefit for the other person?* a. If they try to keep me waiting, I will have to expedite the process with a deadline. b. If they

refuse two offers, I'll tell the salesman the third is a "take it or leave it" offer. There is another dealership not too far down the freeway! I will let the salesman know he might as well make a fast sale and get on to his next customer. He'll make more and save haggling, which earns him nothing. I'm not budging!

6. *How will I bring the process to a conclusion?* I will stand fast by my deadline and my offers.

I used the process, and was fortunate enough to get the car for $300 under invoice!

Knowing your outcome in advance will save you a small fortune in this transaction. In most cases, your OBT process will not be this critical. When you know you are going to enter into a persuasion process, write out on paper the six steps so you can be prepared for what is going to happen. This will ready you for your encounter and give you an edge. Most people don't think before entering into a persuasion situation.

How long will it take you to completely adopt OBT as *your* thinking process? If you write out the six-step process daily, you will greatly enhance your personal power and ability to use OBT within three to four weeks. Like driving a stick shift, you'll feel clumsy at first, then you will become competent as time passes and you use it more. Eventually, you won't even have to implement OBT consciously. It will become your thought process in all your communications.

All CEOs, high-level managers, wealthy entrepreneurs, and top salespeople use OBT. Let's look at how a corporation can use OBT to sell its products.

As mentioned earlier, physical fitness is something that will never go out of style. People like to look good and feel good. Most people will not go out and exercise outside of their homes. Knowing that we live in a world of "couch potatoes," how do we use the OBT process to get people to purchase our expensive ski machines?

1. *What do we (the company) want out of the transaction?* We want to make a nice profit with very few headaches.

2. What does the other person (the couch potato) want? He wants to look good. He wants to feel healthy. He wants people of the opposite sex to find him attractive. He wants to live longer. He wants to feel better about himself. (Essentially he wants to be confident and "desirable.")

3. What is the least we (the company) will accept out of the process? Even though our cost is minimal in the production of these products, it is important to maintain the "integrity" of the price. When we put a product out for sale, we can give away additional incentives for free but we can't lower the price.

4. What problems could come up in the process? a. People will want to return the product because it is hard work for a couch potato to exercise. (The feeling of wishing you hadn't bought something is known as "buyer's remorse.") b. Generic products will compete with us at much lower prices.

5. How will we (the company) deal with each one and, if possible, use the problem as a benefit to the customer (the couch potato)? a. First we offer an unconditional thirty-day money-back guarantee. Even if someone wants to return the product, it is extremely inconvenient to do so as it weighs fifty pounds. It's as easy to keep it and "maybe" use it someday as it is to return it. Second, we tell people how they will feel after those first few workouts. We tell them that for the first week or so they will wish they hadn't bought it but then they'll start seeing results and differences in their bodies. b. The generic products do not have the advertising that we do. Our daily exposure in the newspapers and on TV make the name the product. If people

ask us about price, we simply will respond that our quality is the best. "You take it home and if you don't agree, return it."

6. How will we (the company) bring the process to a conclusion? We will always stand by our product and honor all guarantees to keep the public satisfied, knowing that word of mouth is the best advertising. We will prepare the buyer for the possibility of buyer's remorse.

This of course is a very oversimplified look at selling a product. It *is* the starting point of OBT and that is the issue here. Now you can put this way of thinking to work for you! Whether you want to go out to your favorite restaurant tonight or you are purchasing an expensive new home, this process works.

Key Points Outline: Outcome-Based Thinking

I. Determining your goals

II. Using the OBT process
    A. What do I want out of the process?
    B. What does the other person want?
    C. What is the least I will accept out of the process?
    D. What problems could arise?
    E. How will I deal with each problem, and, if possible,
       turn it into a *benefit* for the other person?
    F. How will I bring the process to a conclusion?

PARADIGM OF PERSUASION

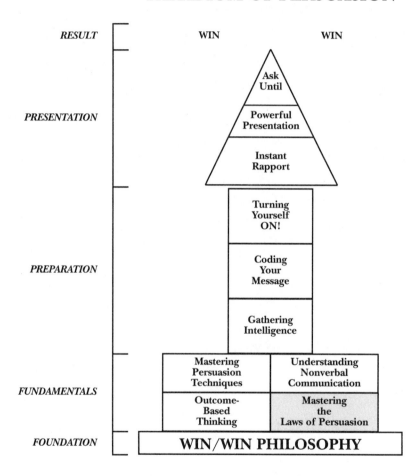

CHAPTER 3

Laws of Persuasion

Opinion is ultimately determined by the feelings, not the intellect.   —Herbert Spencer

If you would win a man to your cause, first convince him that you are his sincere friend.   —Abraham Lincoln

In order to comprehend fully the process of persuasion, we need to understand some basic concepts, or principles, of persuasion. These concepts will provide the foundation for the paradigm of persuasion.

People in each culture develop certain responses to common situations in the persuasion process. These responses to certain stimuli make it possible to predict behavior and therefore persuade others. Unfortunately, it is the same responses that make it possible to manipulate or be manipulated by unscrupulous individuals. Included below are the nine principles that come into play in daily life as well as in persuasion settings, whether you're a salesperson, public speaker, consumer, husband, wife, father, or friend. These are the Laws of Persuasion.

After each law is discussed, examples of behaviors within certain situations will be detailed. These examples are meant to demonstrate the effect the laws of persuasion have on nearly all of us.

Carefully consider each law, recalling a recent conversation or situation where the law came into effect in your life. By doing so you will be able to personalize this powerful information. You will see where you have been manipulated unfairly. You will learn how you have been ethically persuaded. Most important, you will learn how your past behavior has impacted those around you. These laws are the foundation for everything else we will learn about the process of persuasion.

1. Law of Reciprocity

When someone gives you something of perceived value, you immediately respond with the desire to give something back.

(Notice that the law does *not* say that someone will automatically reciprocate when given something. It says he will *desire to give something back.*)

To some degree, reciprocity has control over all of us.

• Each Christmas, millions of people buy gifts and cards for people they probably would never buy for, except that the other person will be giving them something and they *don't want to look bad or feel bad!* From early childhood we were all taught to give something back when something is given to us, generally something of equal value. How often have you been given a gift at Christmas that was more expensive than what you spent on the other person and felt *obligated* to buy something else to *make up the difference* to the other person? This is a powerful example of the law of reciprocity.

• We feel obligated to tip in a restaurant because someone

brought us our food. Our culture trains us to "tip" individuals in some professions (hair stylists, taxicab drivers, waitresses, etc.). Why? Our culture has taught us to do so and that to do otherwise would be considered as rude or unkind.

• Many of us feel obligated to donate to the General Campaign Fund by checking the box on our IRS 1040 tax returns, hoping that that's what they want us to do and we won't then get audited. The fact is, of course, that the IRS is not interested in your political affiliation. It is only interested in the revenue it can bring in for the Treasury Department! The IRS computers do not select returns for auditing on the basis of campaign-fund donations. However, because of the imprinted fear of the IRS that most people tend to have, the campaign fund will continue to do well!

• The bride and groom in a wedding feel obligated to give the bridesmaids and groomsmen gifts because of the expense put up for dresses and tuxedos. In some instances the gift purchased for each person in the wedding party will equal the cost of the tuxedo or dress. Would it not simply be easier to have the newlyweds purchase the dresses and rent the tuxedos?

• A husband feels obligated to work around the house if the wife is doing the cleaning. The poor wife is slaving away, scrubbing the floors, doing the laundry, doing the dishes and everything else that needs doing in the home while the husband watches football, seemingly oblivious. All the while the husband feels guilt, though maybe exhausted himself from a week of hard work. Once again the feeling of *guilt* comes into play in the law of reciprocity.

• Skin care product salespeople will let you have free samples of their products and return ten days later to "see how you liked them and take your order." Most hand lotions will moisturize your skin and, if the fragrance is appealing, there is no doubt the woman trying the free samples for the week will purchase at least *one* of the salesperson's products.

• The neighbor drove the kids to school this week. You'll feel the pressure next week. Each person carries a "favor bank." This is the metaphorical bank we all have for the amount of favors we will do for someone else before needing the bank to be filled back up by the other person. If your favor bank is not refilled, you will feel taken advantage of and eventually will rebel against performing future favors.

• You had a nice dinner with friends across town. You now feel obligated to invite them to your house. Making dinner is a lot of work. Having company over is even more work. To go to someone's house and not then reciprocate will generally make for strained relationships.

• An encyclopedia salesperson will give you a dictionary and thesaurus if you will let her show you the expensive full line. The salesperson will give you a couple of low-cost items in return for a little of your time where you have no obligation to purchase the encyclopedia she wants to show you. The concept is that you are receiving a gift, when of course you are not. It is a trade for your time, which is valuable.

• Large food companies that sell cereal will often send you a free sample in the mail. Next time you go to the store you'll probably buy their brand. Most people purchase the same cereal (or almost anything for that matter . . .) each week. By trying this new cereal, if you like it, you will feel compelled to purchase it at least once.

• Non-profit organizations often will send "stamps" or "seals" with the hope you will use their gifts and send in a small donation. The best gift to compel reciprocity is of course printed return-address labels. No one likes to print his return address on Christmas cards, for example, and therefore a "gift" of address labels will generally provide enough "appreciation" for a five-dollar donation.

You can probably think of many more examples where you have felt obligated or compelled to do things for others because they have done something for you. This is not necessarily "human nature" but it is definitely the result of classical conditioning from early childhood and is very hard to override. Reciprocating, of course, is not necessarily "bad." Clearly, relationships are built on reciprocity. But difficulties occur when reciprocation becomes manipulation.

It is not bad to give gifts to others or accept gifts from others. But it is clear that people dislike the feeling of "owing" or being in a position of repayment. How do you feel when you're in this position? How do you feel when someone has given you a gift? How do you feel when someone has given you a gift at a time of mutual exchange, like Christmas, and you have nothing to give in return?

2. Law of Contrast

When two items are relatively different from each other, we will see them as more different if placed close together in time or space.

Salespeople frequently use the contrast principle because it is so effective.

• "Before we look at the $120,000 home we should look at the $90,000 home." If the two homes are in similar neighborhoods, the more expensive home will have more features the salesperson can use as "hot buttons" and it is the *last* home they will see. People tend to remember the last thing they saw or were told much better than something they were shown or told earlier. If the last home, in this case, is a great deal nicer than the first, then the colorful memory of the nicer home will make the less expensive home seem drab.

• Fund raisers, on the other hand, will use "reciprocal concessions" to meet their goals. For example, if someone wants you to donate $50 to a cause, he will mention that "some people in the community are donating $200, others $100, and those on a tighter budget $50. Which would be best for you?" In other words, if you are told the neighbors are all giving $100, you will feel lucky to get off cheap at $50, won't you?

• Another technique in the category of "reciprocal concessions" is the "money for time" concession. Someone may not have six hours per week to donate to your cause, but coming up with a check for twenty-five dollars won't be too tough to deal with. If you are asked to donate three hours per week to a worthy cause and you clearly don't have the time (and possibly not the desire), then if you can write a small check, you will feel as if you got away with a bargain!

• Retail clothing store sales reps will always sell you the suit first, then offer you "add on" items like socks, sweaters, etc. The additional $20-$60 for the extras is tame compared to the $400 suit. They would never sell you the $60 item first, then try to persuade you to "add on" the suit! After all, what sense does it make to wear a $400 suit and then not buy a beautiful tie for it?

• Restaurant waiters/waitresses will normally take your entire meal order first, then *after* you're done, add on dessert requests. Dessert is cheap compared to the expensive meal you just had.

• Fast-food employees will take your order, *then* mention an additional item: "Would you care for chocolate-chip cookies with that?" This will increase sales 10 percent or more! The one extra item is inexpensive compared to the bill you've just rung up. You will notice they never ask, "Would you like a healthy salad with that, ma'am?" They ask you to buy the cookies that you would not have purchased due to your weight-control program. It is much easier to say yes than say, ". . . and I'll have a package of those chocolate-chip cookies." Why? Because we feel guilty about asking for something we know we shouldn't be eating. We are taught it is polite to accept something when it is offered!

• Once you've purchased the $1,000 couch, isn't it worth $50 for fabric protection? The salesperson will make it perfectly clear that protecting such a valuable investment is simply common sense. (Of course, the salesperson may neglect to tell you that fabric container is sold everywhere at a fraction of the cost and that you could spray it on yourself!)

• Once you've purchased the $10,000 car, isn't it worth $300 for "deluxe rust proofing" or $400 for the super extended warranty? (By the way, did you know many rust-proofing warranty packages only pay off if the rust actually creates a *hole* in the car?)

• An expensive seminar that is a week long may come with a price tag of $5,000. What if you were given a "one time opportunity" to purchase the audio recording of the same seminar for "only $495"? You would receive the same valuable information at *less* than 10 percent of the cost! This is a *perfect* example of the law of contrast.

• Once you've got your new Visa card, isn't it worth $30 per year to register all your credit cards in case of theft and have your monthly payments covered if you become disabled? It *seems* like such a small price to pay in return for the coverage being provided.

You can think of many more cases where, "for just a *little* extra, you can have all these great additional benefits." You can also think of cases where two products remarkably similar in appeal are priced radically different to get you to buy the less expensive one.

Recall the last several times that you purchased a product or service and what items you were asked to buy in addition to your original purchase. Consider the last time that you bought something where you knew there were extras that could have been purchased but were not offered. Why didn't the salesperson offer them to you?

The law of contrast is also used to get you to buy the more expensive product. After all, "the house you *really* want is only $10,000 more than this one, which is OK, but isn't it worth $3 per day to have what you *really* want?" (By the way, with interest, that $3 per day will end up costing you about $30,000!)

3. Law of Friends

When someone asks you to do something and you perceive that person to have your best interests in mind, and/or you would like him to have your best interests in mind, you are strongly motivated to fulfill the request.

People will do almost anything that is asked of them by a friend. Clearly, you *must* be perceived as a friend if you are to be successful in the persuasion process.

The ability to get people to bond to you instantly will be discussed in a later chapter. A few examples of the law of friends are necessary here.

• One winter I coordinated a campaign to raise money for a nationally known nonprofit organization. Instead of hiring hundreds of fund raisers to canvass the Twin Cities, we simply hired fifteen phone callers to contact people by neighborhood.

We called each neighborhood until one person volunteered to be "block worker." All we asked the block worker to do was to take one hour and go door to door requesting donations from his neighbors. The results were phenomenal. A vast majority of block workers did as they promised (we'll talk about the law of consistency later) and because the block workers were soliciting friends, there was no problem with credibility. The organization spent about $10,000 on fund raising and brought in about $70,000 in donations. It is very hard, indeed, to say no to a friend.

• Master Persuaders try to maintain excellent physical appearance. People want to be friends with people who are physically attractive to others. Study after study show that people who are perceived as physically attractive are able to persuade others to give more money and buy more products, and are able to sell a higher percentage of appointments, than those perceived as average in appearance. In addition, we look at good-looking people and believe they are more talented, kinder, more intelligent, and even more honest! Finally, people who are perceived as being attractive are more likely to get lighter jail sentences, get hired, and get paid more. Therefore, the better you let yourself look physically, the more people will want to associate with you, like you, and be your friend.

• Friends are people whom we like and we often like them because they like us. The more we let people perceive we are like them in ideology, philosophy, background, attitudes, etc., the more likely it is we will persuade them. (See chapter 10 for complete information.)

• My grandmother always told me, "Flattery will get you everywhere." She's right. If you can honestly compliment people with *complete sincerity,* you have gone a long way toward becoming their friend.

4. Law of Expectancy

When someone whom you believe in or respect expects you to perform a task or produce a certain result, you will tend to fulfill his expectation whether positive or negative.

• In early January of 1991, Israeli citizens were issued gas masks so that any chemical weapons launched from Iraq would not kill them. When SCUD missiles were fired by Iraq on January 16, 1991, dozens of Israeli citizens checked themselves into hospitals, complaining of symptoms that they were told they would feel after a chemical weapon attack. Interestingly, no chemical weapons were actually used. The law of expectancy is very powerful indeed. This incident is, of course, the opposite of the well-known placebo effect.

• The placebo effect is best described in the following example. The Korean War brought thousands of casualties. Many of these casualties were given placebos (sugar pills and the like) instead of morphine when morphine supplies had run out. In some reports, 25 percent of the soldiers given placebos experienced a significant decrease in pain although no medical reason could be given.

• Small children will often fall and get an "owie." Even minor scrapes will often feel better when Mommy kisses the scrape to make it "feel all better." Children (at least when they're very young!) have a magical illusion that parents can do anything.

5. Law of Association

We tend to like products, services, or ideas that are endorsed by other people we like or respect.

If we like the people connected with a product, we tend to have positive associations in our minds of the product they endorse. Regardless of product quality, because of the endorsement, we often will buy a product the first time based on celebrity endorsement. (The second time around is another story and will be dealt with later.)

• Bill Cosby probably helped you decide to buy Jell-O pudding, Kodak film, and other products. Bo Jackson has sold a world on the idea that Nike tennis shoes are the only way to go. Ray Charles, Michael Jackson, Cindy Crawford and Michael J. Fox have gotten a nation drinking Diet Pepsi. Michael Jordan endorses just about everything and, until he returned to basketball, single-handedly improved the future of minor-league baseball in America!

• Cars are *not* sexy. But a beautiful model describing the newest automobile line can persuade onlookers at auto shows seriously to consider purchasing "her line" of automobile. Logically there is no connection between a "spokes-model" and an automobile. Emotionally and associatively there is a powerful connection in the mind. It is because of emotional and associative reasons that people buy products. We justify those decisions logically.

• Music is one of those amazing things that often brings "triggers" with it. To this day my mother is brought to tears when she hears "I'll Be Home for Christmas." Her brother died in World War II and she was listening to this song on the radio when she heard the news. Music is often linked with romance as well. Many couples have a song they have proscribed as "our song." Those songs will stay with the individuals for years as triggers to memories and emotions that were felt when hearing the music at special times even years earlier.

• During election years, presidential candidates will often quote former presidents of the competing party to document and reinforce their own positions on the issues. This is an excellent tactic often used in presidential debates. Republican candidates will often quote statements of megapopular democrats like John F. Kennedy. This association strikes a positive chord in the minds of all Democrats and former Kennedy supporters. Enough of these associations and the candidate will win a lot of votes on election day.

• Teenagers will normally dismiss an adult's viewpoint on drugs, alcohol, and cigarettes. *But,* when their heroes like Michael Jordan, Charles Barkley, Jay Leno, Arsenio Hall, Hammer, Patrick Swayze, and others flat out state that drugs are stupid, kids listen. We want to be like our heroes. Fortunately, in the early 1990s we had some good heroes for our kids. The likes of Bo Jackson, David Robinson, and other popular athletes taking a stand against drugs had helped reduce the drug intake in America markedly. In school, education programs are well meaning but, for the most part, impotent. If kids associate losers with using drugs, and winners with their heroes who aren't using drugs, the odds are better the kids will stay away from drugs. (It's interesting that as the 1990s move on and the popularity of some role models espousing good values has declined, the use of drugs by teens is rising.)

• The decade of the 1990's will probably be remembered as the "Decade of the Environment." Because of all this "green" thinking, people will become more environmentally conscientious. Manufacturers of products will actually stress the environmental benefits of purchasing their products whether they sell toothpaste, diapers, TV dinners, automobiles, or newspapers. Because of the positive associations in people's minds of helping the environment, consumers will now weigh factors differently in choosing what products to buy.

• The law of association can work the other way around as well. President Clinton in the mid-1990s had to request that many individuals in his administration resign as the public perceived them to be incompetent and not in touch with America. By disassociating himself from these former cabinet and staff members he was largely able to salvage his own image.

6. Law of Consistency

When an individual announces in writing or verbally that he is taking a position on any issue or point of view, he will strongly tend to defend that belief regardless of its accuracy even in the face of overwhelming evidence to the contrary.

• When Pres. George Bush announced, "Read my lips, there will be no new tax increases," he couldn't have guessed how much popularity he would lose when he signed a bill increasing taxes in 1990. When people are perceived as inconsistent, our trust and respect for them decreases markedly.

• Conversely, when Pres. George Bush stated his views on the aggression against Kuwait and that military action could take place on January 15, 1991, there was a split reaction by the general public. On January 16, the president did exactly as he said he would and public opinion in favor of him skyrocketed.

• President Clinton lost a great deal of credibility in the public's eye as he continued to promote policies that were inconsistent with his campaign promises. When people see inconsistency, they start looking elsewhere for solutions, which is why in 1994 the Republicans actually took control of the House and Senate for the first time in over four decades!

• There are literally hundreds of different religious sects under the umbrella called Christianity. Yet, with all of this diversity and the huge sum of literature supporting each sect's point of view, individuals rarely change their denominational affiliations more than once or twice in a lifetime. Many stay within the framework of one denomination their entire lives. When someone says, "I'm a Catholic" over and over throughout his life, it is human nature to be consistent with that commitment throughout that individual's lifetime.

Top salespeople use the law of consistency in very strategic and subtle ways.

MASTER PERSUADER: Do you believe that it is extremely important to cut costs to increase bottom-line profits?

PROSPECT: Sure.

MASTER PERSUADER: If our product could cut your costs and increase bottom-line profits, would you want it?

The Master Persuader did *not* simply ask the prospect the second question, which is what most salespeople do. The Master Persuader asks if certain values are extremely important (i.e., critical, vital, imperative, etc.). Then, when the prospect agrees that a certain thing has *high value,* the Master Persuader offers to give the prospect what he values.

How can the prospect say no? It is very hard indeed to be inconsistent, even when you are communicating with a salesperson you may have just met. The best salespeople, therefore, use the law of consistency in nearly *all* of their presentations.

At home the same strategy can be used as follows:

MASTER PERSUADER: Honey, does it make sense to own better-quality furniture so we don't have to be constantly wasting money on replacing cheap furniture?

HUSBAND: Hm? Yeah.

MASTER PERSUADER: Then should we *invest* in some high-quality furniture this month or wait until next month?

Of course, the husband is virtually obligated to say yes to buying furniture now as the request was so elegantly presented and almost impossible to say no to.

Understanding that people tend to be consistent with past decisions, commitments, and statements, how do we persuade people from a present belief to our way of thinking? People only change if a higher value can be met by changing. (We will discuss values in great detail in a later chapter.) Once you are an "X,", you no longer have to think or make decisions in relation to "X."

As soon as you label yourself, you no longer have to think about it. For someone to take issue with your labels, values, or beliefs creates a great deal of dissonance within you. Your mind is conditioned to fight to be consistent with your commitments whatever they are. Therefore, it is important to get someone to commit to a belief before asking him to become involved in the implication of that belief. (A salesperson will find it important to get the prospect to say that cutting costs is very important to him before asking, "If my product can cut your costs, would you buy it?")

7. Law of Scarcity

When a person perceives that something he might want is limited in quantity, he believes that the value of what he might want is greater than if it were available in abundance.

• I recently went to an electronics/appliance store to purchase a thirty-one-inch television. I wanted the model advertised in the newspaper the preceding Sunday but was still considering other possibilities. After I decided on the model I wanted, I called one of the salespeople over to have him write up my order. He had been watching me carefully comparing televisions for some twenty minutes. I had selected the least expensive of the thirty-one-inch sets. The salesman said he would check to see if it was in stock. He came back out and informed me that "there's one more left—your lucky day." That made me feel fortunate, and iced the sale and a nice commission for his writing my order.

• Television advertisers use the law of scarcity ad nauseam. "While supplies last," "limit two per customer," "offer good Sunday only," "supplies are limited," and "only 10,000 have been minted" are all statements implying scarcity.

• People really believe that the sale at the car dealership will expire this weekend and prices will never be this low again!

• A salesperson who wants an appointment with an executive may use the law of scarcity by implying he has a tight schedule, with certain times or days unavailable, and other alternatives available. "I can't stop by Friday or Monday, but I do have twenty minutes at 3:15 Tuesday. Would that work out for you?"

• An automobile salesperson can use the law of scarcity like this: "Now that you've test-driven the car, do you want the stick shift or automatic transmission? In silver? Hm, this is the last one in stock that is both automatic and silver. If it goes later today, we won't get another like it in stock for weeks. Were you planning on paying cash or financing? Should we go to the finance manager before he leaves for the day?" As you can see, the law of scarcity can also be used in the sense of time. *Two weeks seems like forever* to get the car. You probably want it today and that means you should see the finance manager *now!*

• If you have ever been to a Las Vegas showroom, you know that some seats are prime and very comfortable. Most are cramped to fit the greatest number of people in the show-room. The comfortable booth can be had, however, for a price. A twenty-dollar bill to the maître d' will assure you comfortable seating. A five-dollar tip will get you up front, nearly on top of the stage, and a crimped neck by the end of the show. The good booths are *truly* scarce and in high demand. Because of this, we will pay an exorbitant tip to sit in comfort.

• A young lady who becomes disinterested in her present boyfriend may well gain interest quickly when her boyfriend is paying attention to another young lady. The implied scarcity of the boyfriend gives him much more perceived value.

• My daughter has a complete understanding of the law of scarcity. She can choose from her many toys, books, and dolls for something to play with. Daddy will be reading a boring book with no pictures or colors and what do you think she wants to play with? Daddy's book! At the dinner table, she has her own food and cup. Mommy's food, however, looks much better to her and she will let you know in the dearest of terms.

As with all the laws of persuasion, we will deal with the law of scarcity in more depth when we come to planning our persuasive messages and choosing tactics and strategies.

8. Law of Conformity

Most people tend to agree to proposals, products, or services that will be perceived as acceptable by the majority of other people or a majority of an individual's peer group.

As far as the law of conformity is concerned, people fall into three basic categories:

1. The Conformists
2. The Contrarian Conformists
3. The Contrarian

Conformists make up about 85 percent of all people. They are concerned about how others perceive them and want to be accepted. Conformists are likely to belong to large, accepted groups and organizations.

• Catholics, Lutherans, Republicans, and Democrats are all examples of groups of mass conformity.

• Salespeople need testimonials or letters documenting their claims to show a public of conformists that their decision to buy is a good one. The knowledge that other leaders in a field are using a product or service is very important to a decision maker. Most decision makers are conformists and therefore are more worried about making a bad decision than expecting the benefits of a good decision.

• When one person starts applauding at a concert, the natural urge to applaud with him is nearly unstoppable.

• In 1984, I was fortunate enough to witness a powerful presentation by the Reverend Billy Graham, as he spoke before nearly sixty-five thousand people in Anaheim Stadium. At the end of the program, if you had decided to dedicate your life to Jesus Christ, you could walk out of the stands, down onto the field, and meet with the local church people. The trickle of people at the beginning was slow, then more and more poured onto the field. Eventually, nearly twenty thousand were on the field. The desire to conform was incredible. (Author's note: This is to take nothing away from Dr. Graham. He is one of the most powerful and credible evangelists in the world today.)

Public opinion is very easily swayed. People are desperate to

conform. Like the tide, they rush in together and out together. As a Master Persuader, you are able to use this information in many ways.

Contrarian Conformists make up about 10 percent of all people. Contrarian Conformists tend to rebel against current societal norms in relatively large groups.

• Greenpeace activists and Libertarians are examples of Contrarian Conformist groups.

Contrarian Conformists band together. They set themselves apart from the general population with their views. They then set up their own set of "rules" or beliefs to follow, and thus end up being conformists within their own group.

Contrarians tend to assume Conformists are generally wrong and seldom band together. Entrepreneurs are often Contrarians. Contrarians are not anticonformists like the Contrarian Conformists. Instead, Contrarians use Conformist standards and opinions as information to benefit themselves.

• An example of Contrarian thinking is the use of public opinion in sports betting. In the 1991 Super Bowl, the Buffalo Bills were a 7 point favorite over the New York Giants due to the blowouts of the Los Angeles Raiders and the Miami Dolphins. The line opened at 5½, moved to 6, then to 6½, and finally to 7. Bettors couldn't bet enough money on Buffalo to produce yet another blowout over the Giants. Smart Contrarian bettors jumped on the situation and took the Giants plus the 7 points. They didn't need the 7 as it turned out; the Giants won outright 20-19.

In just about every aspect of life, people will conform to norms for acceptance. Because of this, persuading people using strategies relating to the law of conformity is very easy and effective.

9. Law of Power

People have power over other people to the degree that they are perceived as having greater authority, strength or expertise.

• Physicians wield a great deal of power. When a doctor says something, it is normally perceived to have a great deal of credibility. The degree of power that physicians have over nurses was well documented in the book *Influence,* by Dr. Robert Cialdini. When a doctor phoned a hospital to dispense a drug, even an incorrect one, 95 percent of nurses gave the drug anyway, against hospital policy. That's power!

• Church leaders, especially televangelists, possess a great deal of power over their congregations and viewers. The viewers perceive that the televangelists have "connections in high places," and therefore they can ask almost anything of the viewer and get it.

• College professors have a great deal of power over their students because they determine each student's academic standing.

• Auto mechanics are perceived as powerful by customers. The car is in the mechanic's hands and to the mechanically ignorant, his word is gospel. If he says you need something fixed, you'll probably conform and have it fixed.

• The president of the United States has a great deal of power. He is the commander in chief of the armed services. When the president gives an order, it's followed from the secretary of state to Private Johnson on the front lines. To not follow orders is to ask for serious problems.

• The Internal Revenue Service has a great deal of power. We

are told each year to pay our taxes voluntarily or face tax court.

• The clerk at the post office can't arrest you, or force you to pay your taxes, but he can refuse your package or give you any amount of run around he decides to give you! Clerks in general are powerless people who muster as much power as they can while on the job. Clerks are rule keepers. Rule makers and changers have true power. Rule keepers have only perceived power.

• Threats of violence in cases of noncompliance are also included in this category. Unfortunately, there are still many people who commit abominable crimes with the threat or use of violence in order to get what they want.

When the Master Persuader takes on the persona of a person with great power, he will normally be perceived as powerful by others. How to achieve the persona of power will be discussed at great length later. The more powerful a person is perceived to be, the more likely his requests are to be acknowledged and accepted.

Laws of persuasion can be used for good or bad. An individual's ethics and values will determine how likely he will be to seek WIN/WIN results.

The purpose of this book is to reveal to you all of the significant persuasion laws, techniques, strategies, and tactics. It is the author's greatest hope that you will use this powerful information for your benefit and the benefit of those with whom you communicate.

The laws of persuasion are the foundation of the persuasion process. In the next chapter, you will read about the techniques of persuasion. You will read about the power of questions, the use of secrets and specific words and phrases, nonverbal cues, and deadlines.

The Nine Laws of Persuasion

1. Law of Reciprocity—*When someone gives you something of perceived value, you immediately respond with the desire to give something back.*

2. Law of Contrast—*When two items are relatively different from each other, we will see them as more different if placed close together in time or space.*

3. Law of Friends—*When someone asks you to do something and you perceive that person to have your best interests in mind, and/or you would like him to have your best interests in mind, you are strongly motivated to fulfill the request.*

4. Law of Expectancy—*When someone whom you believe in or respect expects you to perform a task or produce a certain result, you will tend to fulfill his expectation whether positive or negative.*

5. Law of Association—*We tend to like products, services, or ideas that are endorsed by other people we like or respect.*

6. Law of Consistency—*When an individual announces in writing or verbally that he is taking a position on any issue or point of view, he will strongly tend to defend that belief regardless of its accuracy even in the face of overwhelming evidence to the contrary.*

7. Law of Scarcity—*When a person perceives that something he might want is limited in quantity, he believes that the value of what he might want is greater than if it were available in abundance.*

8. Law of Conformity—*Most people tend to agree to proposals, products, or services that will be perceived as acceptable by the majority of other people or a majority of an individual's peer group.*

9. Law of Power—*People have power over other people to the degree that they are perceived as having greater authority, strength, or expertise.*

PARADIGM OF PERSUASION

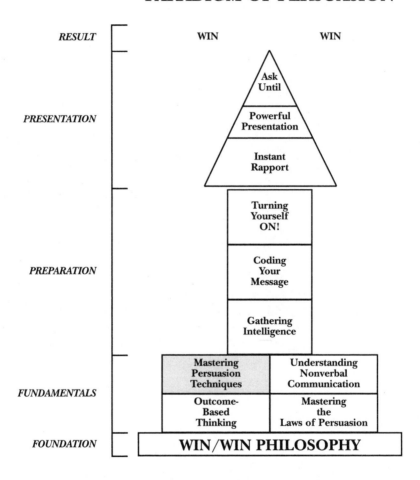

CHAPTER 4

Persuasion Techniques

The object of oratory alone is not truth, but persuasion.
—Lord Macauley

The only way on earth to influence the other fellow is to talk about what he wants and show him how to get it.
—Dale Carnegie

An airplane pilot manipulates the laws of gravity and aerodynamics to successfully move mass quantities of people and machinery thousands of miles in only a few hours' time. The laws are constants.

The same laws pilots use while flying a passenger plane are those Saddam Hussein used in launching SCUD missiles against Israel and Saudi Arabia. He also manipulated the laws of gravity and aerodynamics. The outcome of his endeavor was tragically different from the outcome of a typical airline flight.

Our values tell us that Saddam Hussein is evil and abused the power he had. Similarly, our values tell us that it was morally correct to launch Patriot missiles against the SCUD missiles to protect our allies. An airplane taking off, a SCUD missile launch, a Patriot missile interception: all three use the aforementioned laws of gravity and aerodynamics.

The laws are neither good nor bad. They simply exist. It is how we manipulate, or use, the laws that is good or bad. The laws of persuasion describe, for the most part, how most people respond to a certain set of circumstances.

Persuasion techniques involve the manipulation of the laws of persuasion. They also involve manipulating other current circumstances, which can include the masterful use of questions, sharing secrets, using power words and phrases, applying time pressure, and others.

The Masterful Use of Questions

Questions are valuable tools for the Master Persuader. They are used in the persuasion process to clarify statements, determine values, draw out objections, and direct the conversation. Questions are also used to convince the receiver that your objectives are valid and should be met.

Clarity of Viewpoint

People frequently will respond to your communication in ways that leave their true viewpoints ambiguous. Other times, people don't know what or why they believe what they believe. Therefore, it is necessary to clarify their viewpoints, values, or beliefs to understand how to communicate more effectively with them. This can happen in the sales process, spousal arguments, office meetings, and other areas of communication. Here we look at some examples of dealing with confusion.

If you are a salesperson, you've probably run into this one before. (*MP* denotes Master Persuader.)

RECEIVER: We've got to think it over.

The Master Persuader has a number of options in response to this put-off.

MP A: What precisely was it we needed to consider?

OR

MP B: What did I not cover effectively enough?

OR

MP C: Sure, I understand, you need a few minutes alone. I'll get a cup of coffee and give you some time. Would you like some coffee or a soft drink?

OR

MP D: Do you believe that moving ahead with a positive decision would save you money?

OR

MP E: Please, let me help you, so I understand. Is it the money, or was there something else?

OR

MP F: Before I go, could I leave you some information that would cover your thoughts? What exactly was it you needed to think over?

OR

MP G: Good idea. What would you see as the pluses and minuses of going ahead?

Each option we might choose has a direction in which it will lead the conversation. Let's follow one as an example. Observe how the Master Persuader uses "I'll think it over" to his advantage.

PROSPECT: I really like the car, but I just need to think it over.

MP: I understand. I assume you wouldn't be wasting your time if you didn't feel this was what you wanted. Is that right?

PROSPECT: Well, sure.

MP: Because you're this interested, can I assume you'll give it very careful consideration?

PROSPECT: Of course. What are you getting at?

MP: Well, I thought you might be saying all this just to get rid of me. Are you?

PROSPECT: Of course not.

MP: Is it the integrity of my company?

PROSPECT: No, Kevin, your company is just fine or I wouldn't be here in the first place.

MP: Is it my personal integrity?

PROSPECT: Of course not. I just need a little time.

MP: Hm . . . you must be concerned about the reliability of the car then. Is that it?

PROSPECT: No, I'm telling you I just need a little time. The car is a great car; that's why I'm considering it.

MP: It must be the money! Is that it?

PROSPECT: Well, yes. You see, we may not be able to afford the payments. That's all.

MP: How much were you hoping to be able to handle per month?

PROSPECT: Well, we can't go over $300 a month and this is a $19,500 car. Over sixty months, that works out to more than $300 per month.

MP: Is this the car you really want?

PROSPECT: Yeah, but the payment isn't.

MP: If the payment came to $325 per month, would you settle for less of a car for 85 cents a day?

PROSPECT: I see your point.

MP: Should we go inside?

Did you notice how we went from "I'll think about it" to a $19,500 sale in less than three minutes? Did you notice how every time the Master Persuader said anything, he asked a question? The situation results in a WIN/WIN. Had the buyer been unable to meet the obligation, he would have simply said, "No, I can't do it."

Dealing with Emotional Issues

Questions are used by a Master Persuader to control and lead a conversation with precision. There are times, however, when the use of questions will not lead to a successful change in attitude. This is when the Master Persuader's counterpart is *emotionally involved* in an issue. Masterful use of logic is very important to the Master Persuader. But when the issue is emotionally charged, such as political or spiritual in nature, even precise, logical questions may not be enough to sway a viewpoint. Refer again to the laws of persuasion.

Recall that the law of consistency says, *"When an individual announces in writing or verbally a position on any issue or point of view, he will strongly tend to defend that belief regardless of its accuracy even in the face of overwhelming evidence to the contrary."*

Take, for instance, the example of the man who always buys a certain brand of car. He says it's the best and professes this profusely to anyone who buys another type of car. When he's shown *in writing* that the maintenance and repair record of that car is much worse than other cars of similar size and cost, he will most likely find some reason to dismiss the information and continue believing that *his* car is still the best.

The law of conformity says, "Most people tend to agree to proposals, products, or services that will be perceived as acceptable by the majority of his peer group."

So, if you are a shoe salesperson and you are pushing a new running shoe to a teen who wants Reeboks and nothing else *because all her friends have Reeboks,* you will not be able to sell her the new shoe. Even if the new shoe will last a year longer, stay cleaner, be more comfortable, and be better for the feet, you will have a hard time changing her mind. It is at this point that, regardless of *whether you know that your idea, product, or service will help your prospect, you must let it go.* Even though you would be creating a WIN/WIN situation, it would not be perceived in that manner by the other person.

One final effort to help the prospect would be the question, *"What would I have to do to convince you that taking this action would really help you?"*

If she says, "Nothing," then anything you do from here on out is unethical manipulation and creates a LOSE/LOSE situation.

As a Master Persuader, always keep in mind the laws of persuasion and how they will affect the outcome of your proposal. The laws of persuasion are universal and each law has some affect on all of us.

Each law can be used to the best advantage of both parties. It's your job as Master Persuader to find the WIN/WIN outcome in each encounter.

Clarity of Values

One of the greatest tools of persuasion is to determine a hierarchy of values for yourself and others. It is important to determine both because we tend to assume that everyone has the same values as we do. If we don't clearly know what others' values are, we will tend to assign our own values to the people we communicate with. This makes for poor and even confusing communication, and provides very little chance for successful persuasion.

Let us begin with determining your values. There are two types of values: means values and ends values. Means values are objects or actions. Examples of means values include houses, cars, investments, computers, traveling, marriage, children, sex, sports, boats, fishing, and the like. Ends values are the feelings associated with those means values. Some examples are love, fun, excitement, ecstasy, happiness, security, freedom, action, adventure, peace of mind, success, health, and power.

Under the heading of ends values, there are two categories. Listed above are the *attraction* values. Each person also has a hierarchy of *avoidance* values also. These are *states* that we try to avoid. Included in that list might be depression, sadness, anger, frustration, humiliation, boredom, anxiety, and feeling confined.

You are now ready to determine your values. Without regard to order of hierarchy, simply fill in your most treasured *states* (your *attraction values*), and then your least desired *states* (your *avoidance values*). Do this now.

Attraction Ends Values for Me

_____	_____
_____	_____
_____	_____
_____	_____
_____	_____

Avoidance Ends Values for Me

_____   _____

_____   _____

_____   _____

_____   _____

_____   _____

With that done, let us now create a hierarchy of your *attraction values*. Of all the values you listed, which is *the most* important to you? What is next important to you in life? Then what? Continue until you have completed your hierarchy.

My Hierarchy of Attraction Values

1.   6.
2.   7.
3.   8.
4.   9.
5.   10.

(Examples: love, happiness, security, ecstasy, freedom)

Do the same now for your *avoidance values*.

My Hierarchy of Avoidance Values

1.   6.
2.   7.
3.   8.
4.   9.
5.   10.

(Examples: depression, anxiety, fear, boredom, sickness)

(It should be noted that your values are *not* set in granite. Values can be fluid. My attraction values have changed over the years, as have my avoidance values. These changes do come slowly, of course—in most people, *very slowly!*)

Anthony Robbins, author of the best-selling book *Unlimited Power,* says that we want certain things or conditions in life (means values) because of the *states* we think they will give us (ends values). Therefore, our job as Master Persuader is to show people how they will have their highest values met if they buy our products, donate to our cause, or accept our offer.

How do you find out people's values? *You ask them!*

• CAR SALESPERSON: What's most important in your decision to buy a car?

• ENCYCLOPEDIA SALESPERSON: What's the most important aspect of your owning *Britannica?*

• FUND RAISER: How do you like to see dollars spent by non-profit organizations? Is that the most important way?

• OFFICE MANAGER: What do you like most about your job? What is your most important function?

• HUSBAND: What is most important to you in our marriage?

• FRIEND: What is most important to you in our friendship?

• REAL-ESTATE SALESPERSON: What's most important to you in buying a home? What's next important? Once you own your home, what's most important to you about your home?

If we want to know someone's values, we must ask. Once you know other people's values, you can easily persuade them to whatever result you choose. Herein lies a problem. A Master Persuader seeks a WIN/WIN and nothing less.

Let's say you, Bob, would like to enter into a relationship with Janice. Let's say your highest values include adventure, excitement, and freedom. You, of course, have no idea what her values are. Let's see how the conversation might go on the first date at a formal restaurant.

BOB: I just got back from Los Angeles and will be taking off to London on a big business trip next week. I'm really glad you and I could get together tonight. Do you like the restaurant?

JANICE: It's very nice. I seldom go out to such extravagant places.

BOB: A beautiful woman like you? I find that hard to believe. You know, there is a marvelous restaurant in Paris, on the Seine. Best food I've ever had. I'd love to take you there. Do you travel much?

JANICE: Not much at all. Occasionally, I take a short trip to visit with relatives, my mom and my aunt especially. Nothing like Paris, though.

BOB: Don't know what you are missing! There's so much to see in the world. I can't stand sitting still here in the suburbs all the time. It gets so boring. What do you like to do for excitement?

JANICE: I like to invite friends over and sit in front of the fireplace, sip tea, and just relax. Board games like backgammon are fun once in a while.

These two are destined never to date again. Her values remain a mystery to Bob because he didn't ask her if love, friendship, or security were important. If Bob really wanted more than just one date, he might have approached the conversation like this.

BOB: I just got back from Los Angeles and will be taking off again pretty soon. I can't tell you how excited I was when you agreed to go out with me. Do you like the restaurant?

JANICE: It's very nice. I seldom go out to such extravagant restaurants.

BOB: How do you enjoy spending an evening? I mean, if you could create your perfect evening, what would it be like?

JANICE: Hm, no one ever asked me that before. You mean with two people or with a few friends?

BOB: However you decide. It's *your* perfect evening!

JANICE: Well, I'd have a few friends over to my place. We'd sit in front of the fireplace and sip on tea, maybe a glass of wine, talk about what's going on in our lives. There would be soft instrumental music in the background; the porch light would be on outside so you could see the snow falling through the window. The Christmas tree would be lit and the other lights dim. And . . . well, I could go on and on.

BOB: You obviously like Christmas. Is that right?

JANICE (smiling): Best time of year. Everyone is so friendly to everyone else. There's such a positive spirit. You know what I mean?

BOB: I love Christmas, too. I was in the Swiss Alps at Christmastime last year.

JANICE: Did you miss being with your family?

BOB: I sure did, but I must say I had a wonderful week of skiing.

Now, Bob and Janice may not get married based upon this conversation, but Bob now understands Janice a lot more than he did when they walked in the door. He also knows what kinds of things are important to her. Bob in the second scene is finding out about Janice. In the first, he is telling about himself. Needless to say, the second scenario will be much more effective in creating a friendly relationship and the opportunity for a second date.

It is critical to understand what values people have. The only way to find out is to ask.

Learning people's values should be practiced in all relationships, both personal and professional. Salespeople need to learn the values of their clients before attempting to meet their needs with specific products. Remember this: *prescription before diagnosis is grounds for malpractice.*

We should not persuade people to our idea, product, service, or belief unless it is in their best interest.

Power Words

Words are only a small part of the communication process. In fact, you will learn in the next chapter how small a part words play compared to nonverbal communication. Nevertheless, some words do have a powerful impact on those you are attempting to persuade.

The Name

The most powerful word on the face of the earth is our own name. When you were a baby, you heard your name over and over again. You linked it with getting attention and you very much liked that. Most people have a first, middle, and last name. Which were you identified by? That is the name that has the persuasive edge with you. I developed a fondness for all three of my names. For most people, however, it is the first name that carries impact.

Salespeople who try to use this technique by referring to a prospect as Mr. Johnson, or Ms. Rogers, normally come off sounding like pitchmen. The effect is negligible and indeed often hurts their presentation.

On the other hand, research has shown that if you use a person's first name, at the very beginning or the very end of a sentence, the likelihood of persuading that person is drastically increased. This, of course, does *not* mean one needs to inanely repeat someone's name over and over to make a sale, win an argument, or get a date.

Proper use of names is illustrated below.

• "John, do you think we could go out tonight?"

• "If our new computer software can save you over two thousand dollars in secretarial time this year, would you want it, Jane?"

• "Bill, would you be kind enough to expedite the budget analysis?"

• "This car will make you look pretty good in it, don't you think, Keith?"

The use of a person's name is a powerful attention getter and it also acts in a highly positive associative manner with whatever statement or request is linked with it.

Please and Thank You

Please and thank you are the next in line to a person's name in giving the Master Persuader the persuasive edge. Like our name, these words have been taught to us since we were children. We were taught that we will get something if we say please and, once we have it, we must say thank you. Therefore, when these terms are used in communication, they carry a great deal of impact.

Proper use of these terms in the persuasive process is illustrated in the following examples:

• "Thank you for seeing me today."

• "Please give this proposal every consideration, John."

• "Thank you for coming to Bob's Autos. I believe you'll find our staff remarkably service oriented. Please ask for any help you need."

• "Please, give what you can."

• "Please let me help you isolate your financial needs so we can come to a mutually beneficial proposal."

Because

The fourth most powerful term in the English language is "because." When you were young, you were told over and over, "Because I said so." These words carried authoritative weight. As adults, a more refined "Because" carries just as much authoritative weight.

Ellen Langer, a Harvard social psychologist, performed a fascinating experiment in 1977. She asked a favor of people waiting in line to use the library's copy machine. When she asked, "Excuse me, I have five pages. May I use the machine, *because I'm in a rush?*" 94 percent let her move ahead in line!

When the request was phrased without those last five words,

only 60 percent let her move ahead in line. Most fascinating of all, however, was that when she asked, "Excuse me, I have five pages. May I use the machine *because* I have to make some copies?" 93 percent let her move ahead in line with no reason other than *because!* You should definitely use the word "because" in your persuasive efforts.

• "Because of the amount of money you'll make, you'll want to invest now."

• "You'd probably be happiest investing in the largest advertisement available because of the increased response you'll get."

The addition of this word to your persuasive vocabulary will take conscious effort. Your time investment will pay off dividends many times over.

There are many terms like the four discussed above that are powerful in the persuasion process. Salespeople of all kinds will find the following list especially helpful.

Thirty-two Power Words That Sell

Advantage	Exciting	Improved	Proud
Save	Deserve	Discovery	Easy
Benefit	Fun	Investment	Proven
Security	Guarantee	Happy	Health
Comfort	Free	Joy	Profit
Trust	Love	Money	New
Results	Right	Safety	Truth
Value	Powerful	Vital	You

Time-Pressure Techniques

Some people are simply slow at making decisions. It is often important to the Master Persuader to move the process along. It would be wise to keep in mind the law of scarcity: *"When a person perceives that something he might want is limited in quantity, he believes that the value of what he might want is greater than if it were available in abundance."*

For 2,000 years, church leaders have used time-pressure techniques very effectively. The leaders instruct their congregations to act morally, evangelize more, lead better lives, and, yes, give more to the Church *because* the return of the Messiah is imminent. The technique is very effective. As we approach a new millennium and as tensions in the Middle East continue to heat up, who knows, this may be the year!

Nonprofit organizations are masterful at using time-pressure techniques. If the public doesn't act now to support causes, the death of children, adults, even the environment can occur. Your support, the public is told, will prevent the terrible things from happening. If you give today, it is virtually assured. Tomorrow may be too late. At least for one child, they say.

A couple of years ago, I bought an entire set of encyclopedias from Britannica. I was recently told by an encyclopedia salesman that I should buy the additional set of "Great Books" *now* because prices would soon be going up. It wasn't enough to sell me. Had he offered me $100 off the retail price and interest-free financing if I bought today, I might have gone for the books!

If you are going to buy into something like time sharing, realize that, for the salesperson, there is no tomorrow. Therefore, the salesperson must be prepared to offer whatever it takes to make the sale. Knowing this, the prospects that are truly interested should not sign on the dotted line right away. Allow the salesperson to come down and down and down. Don't be afraid to offer an incredibly *low* price for your week of time sharing. Many developers will take your offer so they can announce to the rest of the prospects in the room that you are the proud new owners of a week of time sharing.

The more time you spend with any salesperson, the more

he is pressured to offer his product to you at the lowest price possible. Time is money. If you spend five to six hours with a salesperson, he will feel compelled to make any kind of a deal with you that he can.

Master Negotiator Herb Cohen says, "I care, but not that much." If you can assume that attitude and realize that life and death aren't involved in this particular persuasion process, you'll be more relaxed and less pressured. If you can walk away and say *no* when the deal turns from WIN/WIN to LOSE/WIN, you will do well.

If you are a salesperson who works by appointment with businesspeople, especially those in retail, here is a golden nugget for you: Friday is the busiest retail day of the business week. Therefore, set your appointments on Friday, a day when the store owners are very busy and have little time to "dig into" your product or service on the phone. You can let them know that you know they are busy and will stop by to fill them in on the details on Tuesday. They will generally appreciate this, and on most early-week appointments will have the time to sit and talk to you face to face.

Remember, time can be either an asset or a liability. The person who needs something the fastest will normally pay more than the person who can wait. One-hour film developing can cost from 50 to 100 percent more than two- to three-day developing. Eyeglasses ground in one hour will cost double those that need to be sent to a main laboratory. When time is something we don't have a lot of, we will pay for it!

In negotiations of all kinds, if you are under no time pressure, you probably have little to lose. When this is the case, you needn't worry. All the pressure will be on the other party.

Time pressure relates to all aspects of persuasion as we can see. The next technique we describe will very likely surprise you.

Credibility Techniques

It never ceases to amaze me how often people who are

honest and have high integrity are perceived as untruthful in high-powered communications settings. Indeed, the opposite is also true. The dishonest and crooked are often perceived as truthful and people of high integrity.

Why is this? Credibility is in the eye of the perceiver. We will not be perceived as credible if we don't meet our perceiver's standards.

The law of persuasion to keep in mind here is the law of friends: *"When someone asks you to do something and you perceive that person to have your best interests in mind, and/or you would like him to have your best interests in mind, you are strongly motivated to fulfill the request."*

The first rule of credibility is never to tell another person more than he can believe. Your product, service, or idea may be the best there is and solve all the problems in the world. But if the perceiver doesn't think it can do all this and more, he won't want anything to do with it or you. You will be perceived as exaggerating and this will result in a LOSE/LOSE situation.

You must be ready to point out the negative aspects of your service. Even IBM has bad points! (Not many, but they are there.)

If you can point out a negative aspect about your product, service, or idea, you'll disarm the perceiver from trying to find it, leaving him to focus on the benefits. You gain great credibility when you appear objective looking at your own products, services, ideas, and opinions.

The second thing you can do to appear credible is to be precise. Instead of saying that you lost twenty pounds, say the truth. You lost seventeen pounds! That sounds 100 percent believable.

A famous example of precision is Dove soap advertising itself as 99 44/100 percent pure. Now, I doubt that if you chemically broke it down you would come up with 99 44/100 percent pure. It's probably *more*. But that number sounds exactly right, doesn't it? You would never question it.

If your computer software will save a company 28 percent, say it will save them 28 percent. Don't say 30 percent.

Products or services that sell for $500 give the appearance of a negotiable price, but those that sell for $497 appear to have a less negotiable price.

Another key step in gaining credibility is to have written documentation by objective parties. *You* can say something to make a sale and it may be suspect. For someone *else* with nothing to gain from the transaction to say something incredible about you or your product is a *big* credibility builder.

Finally, in most transactions the person who started the transaction probably has something to gain. It would be very wise to diminish that fact: "Whether you buy my product or not is OK with me. It's either going to make a big difference for you, or it isn't. If it's not, you shouldn't buy it. It's completely *up to you.*" After you've said that, all defenses come down and you will generally be perceived as a professional, competent, and credible salesperson.

If you are not in sales, credibility is still a very important part of who you are. Are you a person of your word? Are you 100 percent reliable, 100 percent consistent, 100 percent of the time? Do you always come through? Do you walk your talk? Are you always seeking WIN/WIN situations? If so, you will be perceived as credible in your business and personal relationships.

Secrets

Nearly everybody loves secrets. When you share secrets with people, you gain a great deal of trust from your listeners.

• "I shouldn't be telling you this, but . . ."

• "Can you promise me you won't say anything to anyone about what I'm going to tell you?"

• "Off the record, I think you should know . . ."

- "I'm not supposed to tell anyone about that, but here's how it works . . ."

Statements like these show that you are confiding in your listener. When you confide in people, you tend to get reciprocal behavior. Once communication is completely open on intimate levels, persuading your counterpart is a very simple outcome to achieve.

Future Pacing

A good salesperson is always "closing." Great salespeople use "future pacing." The questions below are examples of future pacing.

- "If you like our product, will you buy it again?"

- "If you like our service, will you let us handle all of your needs in this area?"

Future pacing requires that the prospect buy your product today, or the prospect would not be able to determine whether he should use your product or service again. When you have used the future pacing technique, and the prospect has conditionally told you he will use your product or service again, generally speaking he has agreed to try your product once.

At this point, many salespeople "buy it back"; they continue to sell when the prospect has already bought. This invariably brings skepticism to the prospect's mind and makes it look as though you're justifying your product. Don't "buy it back." Once he's bought your product or service, let him have it—do the paperwork!

Hypnotic Language Patterns

One of the most powerful tools an individual has is the precise and influential use of language. In hypnotherapy, the practitioner's job is to set the client at ease, help him relax, and carefully convince him that he can achieve whatever goals that he has come to the practitioner for.

Although it takes a great deal of practice to learn the dynamics of hypnosis, one can quickly learn a few of the more valuable hypnotic language patterns. Have you ever noticed that certain persuasive people are so "soft sell" that you are amazed they sell anything, yet they do quite well?

"Don't" Language Patterns

We know that people cannot make a picture of the word "don't" in their minds. More specifically, a picture cannot be made of "don't" because it is not a noun. Therefore we can use this word in language patterns to influence others. Here are a few examples:

- "Don't feel as though you have to buy something today."

- "Don't look at me and smile."

- "Don't consider taking me out to dinner if you don't want to."

- "Don't decide now. You can do it later if you're uncomfortable."

- "You don't have to help me clean the house . . . really."

- "I don't know if this book is going to completely change your life."

• "Don't make up your mind too quickly."

Go back to each of these sentences, delete the word "don't," and you will get the message that the unconscious mind is getting. The reason why so many children disobey is that they frequently hear the word "don't." The brain skips over the word "don't" as it is not a noun or verb that can be pictured. The brain goes straight to the rest of the message and then it *might* return to the word "don't" by negating the entire message. More often than not, when handled in this specific manner, this language pattern is very powerful.

The word "don't" will be dealt with again later in this book in a slightly different context. Please write down seven sentences, like those above, where you want someone to do something but want to soften the request with the word "don't." Do this before continuing to the next set of hypnotic language patterns.

Might and Maybe Language Patterns

Most individuals use language patterns that are far too explosive or demanding in the persuasion process. This mistake is common across our culture. We tend to give orders to our spouses, children, and employees. We do *not* like to take orders and resent them when we hear them. Therefore, we can use "Might and Maybe Language Patterns" to help us persuade others in a far more gentle and effective way.

• "You might want to take the trash out . . . now."

• "You might want to cut the lawn . . . now."

• "You might want to consider adding to your portfolio . . . now."

• "You might want to take me out to dinner tonight/now . . ."

• "You might want to buy this book . . . now."

• "You might notice your feelings toward me will change with each passing day/now . . ."

• "You might notice how good you feel when you drive down the street in this beautiful new vehicle."

• "You might not have noticed how many people already own this car today."

• "You might not have noticed how many people are involved in civic clubs."

• "Maybe you haven't purchased more life insurance yet."

• "Maybe you'll see some special snack at the grocery store that you can bring home for me."

• "Maybe you'll go ahead with the investment program when you consider your future, tonight."

These patterns are similar to those of the Don't Language Patterns. Go to each of the statements above and delete the words "might" and "maybe." Notice that once again the statements are all commands without the words "might" or "maybe." Also notice the gentleness of these commands with the words "might" and "maybe."

Before continuing you *might* want to write out seven examples of each of the above patterns. Then feel free to continue to the next set of language patterns.

Assumption of the Obvious Language Patterns

When we give people credit for knowing something they really know nothing about they generally will say nothing and allow us to believe them to be smarter or more aware than they really are. Think about that for a moment.

Once we realize how important this is in understanding human behavior we can then bring the concept into the persuasion process in a very elegant manner. In each pattern below, the assumed knowledge word or phrase is italicized.

• "*You probably already know* that you'll feel better when you quit smoking."

• "*You probably already know* that you're going to buy this."

• "*You probably already know,* deep in your heart, how much I love you."

• "*People can, you know,* lose weight with this plan."

• "*People can, you know,* make a mistake without trying to hurt someone."

• "You will *realize* how smart you have been for having purchased this book."

• "You will soon *realize* that you have made the right decision to join our church."

• "*Sooner or later* you will know that this is the right church home for you."

• "*Sooner or later* you will be happy with your decision."

• "*Eventually,* you will know that this is right for you."

• "*Eventually,* you may notice how happy I make you."

I'm sure you realize how important these "Assumption of the Obvious Language Patterns" really are. You probably already know that I'm going to ask you to write seven sentences using each of these patterns so you will reap the benefits of this technology. Please do so before continuing to the next set of patterns.

Tell You Language Patterns

People do not like to be told what to do. We like to think that each great idea is ours and that when we have a great idea, it is entirely our own. This means that the Master Persuader will always want to "frame" his language in such a way that prospects will not disagree, especially on important or controversial issues.

• "*I wouldn't tell you* to leave your religion *to* join mine, *because* I always want your respect and I know you will make the right decision."

• "*I wouldn't tell you* to consider a new career, *because* you want to be in charge of your own future."

• "*I could tell you that* you are making a mistake *but* I won't. You want to figure it out for yourself."

• "*I could tell you that* Toyotas are far superior to this car *but* I won't. You'll realize it after you've owned this car for a few years."

I could tell you to write seven sentences to embed these patterns firmly in your mind, but I'm sure you know by now how important they are, so I won't. Please continue with the final pattern we will learn in this chapter when it is appropriate.

The Truth Language Pattern

Truth is what each individual believes it to be. Ask someone if he belongs to the true church or is in the true religion. Ask him if the people in his political party tell the truth. The people you come into contact with every day often want to know if you are being truthful with them. This most often occurs in the selling process but is applicable in any persuasive communication setting. The way someone knows you are telling the truth is if you believe the same thing he does. If you agree with him, then you also are right and are telling the truth. "The Truth Language Pattern" is not only an excellent hypnotic language pattern used in therapy; it is also powerful for getting people to agree with you on just about anything.

The key to this pattern is to get someone to either say or think, "Yes, yes, yes, yes," then request what you desire.

"Taxes are too high!"
"The deficit is skyrocketing!"
"Crime is on the rise!"
"Your money is being misspent by the government!"
"You are sick of the current administration!"
(Therefore)
"Vote for me and we will make a change together!"

"You want to feel as though you will have money to live comfortably in your retirement."
"You deserve the best things in life."
"You've sacrificed for your children."
"You've worked hard all these years."
(Therefore)
"Invest in this program to give you not only what you have earned, but what you deserve."

"I've worked every day without a complaint."
"I do all the housework."

"I take care of the kids."
"I do the books every month."
(Therefore)
"Don't you feel I deserve this one-week vacation?"

By getting the "yes, yes, yes, yes" response either verbally or internally, you create a receptive state of mind in the person you are trying to persuade. Once the person is in this state, it is very difficult for him to say no after saying yes to so many statements or questions.

You've noticed how important writing seven statements has been to you, haven't you? You've seen the value of not just learning these patterns, but knowing them, right? You know that by using these patterns you will be a happier person, right? Then would now be a good time to write down seven examples of the Truth Language Pattern?

Because of the power of persuasion techniques, it once more needs to be stressed that our goal is WIN/WIN and nothing less.

Key Points Outline: Persuasion Techniques

I. The Masterful Use of Questions
   A. Clarity of Viewpoint
   B. Dealing With Emotional Issues
   C. Clarity of Values
      1. Attraction Means/Ends Values
      2. Avoidance Means/Ends Values

II. Power Words
   A. Name
   B. Please and Thank You
   C. Because

III. Time-Pressure Techniques

IV. Credibility Techniques

V. Secrets

VI. Future Pacing

VII. Hypnotic Language Patterns
    A. "Don't"
    B. Might and Maybe
    C. Assumption of the Obvious
    D. Tell You
    E. The Truth

PARADIGM OF PERSUASION

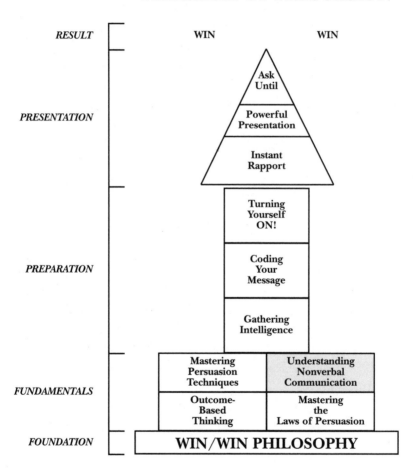

CHAPTER 5

The Impact of
Nonverbal Communication

Actions speak louder than words.   —Anonymous

We are always communicating. Even as we sit in silence, we communicate with those around us. The way we walk sends a message to others. The way we smile, sit, and rest all send messages out to those around us. There is no such thing as "not communicating."

When someone says, "That's it, I'm not talking to you anymore!" he is communicating. The message is one of anger or some other negative emotion. He may think he has stopped communicating when in reality he is communicating very loudly! It's no longer verbal, of course, and that is what we will discuss in this chapter.

Interestingly, the nonverbal communication we exhibit is two to seven times more significant in the persuasion process than the words we say. As we become more skilled in effective communication, we must become excellent nonverbal communicators.

In this chapter, we will learn the importance of our nonverbal communication and its impact on others. We will learn where to sit or stand when involved in the persuasion process, how to sit, how to move, and how close to others we need to be in order to influence them. We will also learn the importance of our appearance, when to smile, and when not to smile. Finally, we will learn the importance of nonverbal cues and how to be sure that our verbal message is congruent with our nonverbal message.

Let's begin with a simple but important exercise. Read each sentence below stressing the italicized words. Notice the significant difference in the meaning of each sentence.

1. *He's* giving this money to John.
(*He* is the one giving the money, no one else.)

2. He's *giving* this money to John.
(He is *giving*, not lending, the money.)

3. He's giving *this* money to John.
(*This* money, not any other.)

4. He's giving this *money* to John.
(Not his credit cards or checks but *money*.)

5. He's giving this money to *John*.
(*John* is getting the money, not Kevin or Fred.)

The stress on a particular word can change the entire focus of the communication process. If our vocal message contradicts our verbal statement, we are probably being sarcastic.

YOU: Are you having fun?
ME: Won-der-ful [stated slowly and clearly].

Now that is sarcastic. The vocal message is much more important than the verbal one. If we are perceived as being sarcastic at an inappropriate time, not only do we stifle communication, but we destroy our ability to influence.

A study conducted by Mehrabian in 1967 pitted vocal cues against facial ones and found the facial more influential. From these studies, Mehrabian devised a formula that illustrates the impact of verbal, vocal, and facial cues:

perceived attitude = 7 percent verbal + 38 percent vocal
+ 55 percent facial

It should be noted that the percentages don't necessarily hold up in every kind of interaction. But the point is clear. Our nonverbal behavior makes up about 60-90 percent of our message.

Ray Birdwhistell, a pioneer in nonverbal research, says that in a normal two-person conversation, the verbal components carry less than 35 percent of the social meaning of the situation. More than 65 percent is carried on the nonverbal band.

In a persuasive communication setting, the value of the words we speak is about 15 percent of the overall message. Vocal cues, including rate, tone, pitch, volume, and emphasis, are valued at about 35 percent. Physiology, including facial expression, posture, body movement, and eye contact, would rate at about 50 percent. We cannot place exact percentages on each of the three categories. This is one reason why persuasion is an art and not a perfect science.

All communication is related to the context it is occurring in. The value of specific language is greater on the phone than it is face to face. When you speak to someone who is blind, the timbre, tone, and cadence of speech are far more important than your appearance. Being aware of your context is just one aspect of the communication process. One way to study our context is through the science of proxemics.

Proxemics and Persuasion

The first factor we need to consider in the persuasion process is called proxemics. Proxemics refers to the space in which we communicate. There are three kinds of space that we will discuss.

1. *Fixed-Feature Space*—Organized by unmoving boundaries like rooms in houses or buildings.
2. *Semifixed-Feature Space*—Includes the arrangement of moveable objects like tables, chairs, and other furniture.
3. *Informal Space*—This is like a series of "bubbles" around each person.

Fixed-Feature and Semifixed-Feature Space

The owner of the fixed-feature space has an overwhelming advantage in the persuasion process. In sports, this is called the home-field advantage. There is a certain advantage when you do just about anything in your own territory as opposed to other areas. In the persuasion process, the home-field advantage is also very important. If you can negotiate in your office, your building, your home, your yard, or your normal environment, you have a clear edge and should do so if possible. As soon as you are on someone else's turf, you are at a great disadvantage. The surroundings are different, you are less comfortable, and your odds at being successful in your objective are decreased.

If you are a salesperson, you must learn to "blend in with the woodwork." This is much easier said than done. In order to become at ease in other "nonfriendly" environments, you must learn to see how other people act in the environment. Are things tense and the people rigid, or are they casual and relaxed? Adapt to your environment like a chameleon.

If the meeting place is owned by your counterpart, you can begin to see, with a quick scan of the walls and decor, what he is proud of. You may or may not choose to comment on his personal property. If you are new to the persuasion arts, simply soak up the surroundings and stick to your business. If you are moderately successful in the art of persuasion, comment on mutual interests.

If you are not in a formal office, you may have some control over seating. Seating arrangements are *very* important to the persuasion process.

Rectangular tables—If you seek conversation, compare the following.

```
      X            X           XX
X  [    ]        [    ]       [    ]
                   X
  Good           Good          No
```

If you seek cooperation:

```
      X            X           XX
 X [    ]        [    ]       [    ]
                   X
  Good            OK          Best
```

Square or round tables—If you seek conversation:

```
   X                          X
 X[ ]                        [ ]
                              X
  Good                        No
```

If you seek cooperation:

```
   X                          X
 X[ ]                        [ ]
                              X
  Good                        No
```

In a bar or nightclub with—

	X X □	X □ X	XX □
Same-Sex Friend	Best	OK	Good*
Opposite-Sex Friend	Best	Good	No
Intimate Friend	Good	OK	Best

*Female/female only

At a restaurant with—

	X X □	X □ X	XX □
Same-Sex Friend	No	Best	OK*
Opposite-Sex Friend	Good	Best	No
Intimate Friend	OK	Best	Good

*Female/female only

Leadership seating—1, 3, and 5 denote frequent talkers, 2 and 4 denote noncommunicators, 1 or 5 is a task-oriented leader, and 3 is a socioemotional leader (like President Clinton) concerned about group relationships, getting everyone to participate:

```
       1
     ┌───┐
     │   │ 2
     │   │ 3
     │   │ 4
     └───┘
       5
```

These charts will help you in determining how to use semi-fixed space. Using seating arrangements rated as *Best* or *Good* will greatly enhance the persuasion process. Making people feel uncomfortable or using seating arrangements unfavorable to conversation or cooperation will decrease the likelihood of WIN/WIN communication.

Informal Space

The more comfortable you make your counterpart feel, the more likely he will trust you. This will increase the chances for closing the persuasion process with a WIN/WIN result.

You should be aware of two factors in particular in the use of informal space. The first is the distance between communicators and the second is touching your counterpart.

In *The Hidden Dimension,* by Edward T. Hall, we learn that informal space is classified into four categories:

1. intimate	0-18 inches
2. casual-personal	1.5 feet-4 feet
3. social consultative	4 feet-12 feet
4. public	12 feet-limit

When you are attempting to persuade someone with whom you are not intimate, you need to keep out of the intimate range or "bubble" of 0-18 inches. Men influencing men would be wise to work within a 3-foot to 6-foot range. Women working with women should be in the casual-personal zone of 1.5 feet-4 feet. Women influencing men should be in the casual-personal zone as well. The complex model is when men are influencing women, which can range from 2 feet to 8 feet depending upon feedback.

Once again, please remember that these are general guidelines for the general population. There are individual differences. This will give you a starting point.

The second factor to consider is that of touching. Touching should be avoided in most cases if the persuasion process is within the ranks of a manager/employee or employer/employee relationship. These days there is a fine line between a friendly tap on the arm and sexual harassment.

In intimate relationships, touching is *very* important. It is also important in the persuasion process. We will focus our attention on settings including sales, friendly persuasion, and social situations.

The notion of touch is important because the correct use of touching will, in most cases, bring about a positive result. First, let us consider acceptable places we can touch most people in today's society in the persuasion process.

Men by Men	*Women by Women*
hand	hands
shoulder	forearm
forearm	upper arm
upper arm	knee

Women by Men	*Men by Women*
hands	virtually entire body
forearm	

The above chart is valuable. Most people will be comfortable with touch in each category as stated. The ideal way to use touch is immediately before your key point. Take your pointer finger and middle finger and touch the forearm of your counterpart. Hold for one to three seconds while looking at him or her in the eye, state your point, and ask for agreement. You may use this touch one more time at the close of your communication and no more. If the touch was effective the first time, the exact repetition will most likely trigger a positive response to your offer and result in a WIN/WIN situation.

Strategic Movement

The most powerful nonverbal process you can use with an audience is that of "strategic movement." When giving his nightly monologue for some twenty-seven years Johnny Carson always stood in exactly the same place on stage. There was a star in the studio to mark the spot where Johnny would begin his monologue. Over time, as you watched "The Tonight Show," you knew precisely where Johnny was going to and you were prepared to laugh. The only thing Johnny did from this star was make people laugh. As an audience, we became "anchored" to him making us laugh while standing on the star.

Because the entire study and creation of strategic movement could fill a book itself, here we will simply give a brief example. It is a very complex area difficult to master, yet very powerful. The following scenario will give you a flavor of this largely unknown field.

If you are called on to make a speech or give a presentation, you want to select three points on the stage from which to speak. The first point is where you will do most of your talking. We will say that this is point "A" and is a podium. There will also be a "Bad News Point," which we will call "B." It is at point "B" that we will talk about anything that is negative or bad in any way. It is from point "B" that *all* bad news comes. When we have something wonderful, something grandiose, something exciting, to tell our audience, we go to the other side of the stage and speak from point "C." Everything we want the audience to agree with or like is said from here. We always talk about good things from this point. This is the "Good News Point."

Here is how you use strategic movement. Imagine that you are giving a speech at a fund-raising dinner for your favorite charity. Your job is to get the people to donate in a big way. You begin your speech at point "B." You begin to discuss how bad things are. You tell everything negative about whatever it is your charity is trying to help. You only discuss the negative impacts of the social problem that you are trying to stop. You have clearly established "B" as the "Bad News Point" in people's minds although they will never become conscious of it, unless they read this book!

Now after you have laid out the problem at its absolute worst, you move directly to point "C," where you will become excited at how this charity will solve the problems noted at "B." You will excite the audience; you will tell them how sharp they are for being here tonight. You will "anchor" everything "grand" to point "C."

The core of the speech will be informational of course and will take place from the podium (point "A"). This is our neutral point.

When it comes to the end of your speech you will once again make a memorable demonstration at point "B" as to the seriousness of the problem and then go all the way over to point "A" and solve the problem.

The most exciting part of this strategy is the question and answer session after the speech.

A person asks if giving to "a competing charity" might also be a good idea. You walk to point "B" and say something like this:

"Well, of course you know that charity is a good charity and there would be nothing wrong with that . . . of course . . . [walking to point 'C'] by taking advantage of the plan that we have we can accomplish all of the goals that you want to see accomplished in the community. I'm sure you realize it's up to you to make it happen. We can only help those who need it if you make a decision tonight."

By discussing the other charity in a neutral or slightly positive way from the "Bad News Point," you associate it with the problem while stating that it is a good charity. The nonverbal and verbal messages will cancel each other out. By moving to the "C" point when you are answering the question with the goal in mind of raising money tonight, you associate your charity with all that is good and solution oriented.

There is no more powerful use of space than that of "strategic movement." When you are watching someone on TV sell something, especially in the infomercials, watch carefully for strategic movement.

Strategic movement was one of the best-kept secrets in communication, until you read about it in this book!

Physical Appearance

An attractive physical appearance is likely to enhance your persuasion capabilities greatly. A number of studies support this conclusion.

• In studies done at college campuses, it has been proven that female students perceived by faculty as attractive receive substantially higher grade-point averages than male students or unattractive females (studies by J. E. Singer).

• In studies related directly to the persuasion process, it has been found that attractive females could change attitudes of males more than unattractive females could (studies by Mills & Aronson).

• Dating and marriage decisions are often made with great weight placed on attractiveness. A wide variety of research has shown that men will reject women lacking (in their opinion) good looks, disposition, morals, and health. Women have proven to be less concerned about looks (studies by R. E. Baber).

• As far as strangers are concerned, individuals perceived as deficient in physical attractiveness are undesirable for any kind of an interpersonal relationship (studies by D. Byrne, O. London, K. Reeves).

• In a study by Brislin & Lewis, fifty-eight unacquainted men and women were studied in a social setting. After a first date, 89 percent who wanted a second date decided to do so because of attractiveness of the partner.

The point is simple. Every study available on physical attractiveness reveals that people who are perceived as attractive (especially women) are also perceived as more likable, intelligent, trustworthy, and credible than unattractive people. It may seem "plastic" or "shallow," but it is a reality.

Obviously, the Master Persuader must enhance his or her physical appearance. The following are obligatory:

1. Appropriate dress for your persuasive setting. (Molloy's *New Dress for Success* is highly regarded for businesspeople.)

2. A neat appearance in every way from hair to shoes.

3. Positive body smell. *Not* overly perfumed.

4. No breath odor.

5. In style for those who will be looking at you.

6. Controlled weight.

One piece of research available indicates that in over half of all instances, managers decide whether or not to hire someone before the interviewee opens his or her mouth. Physical appearance is very *important!*

Look in the mirror and ask yourself, "What can I do to improve my physical appearance?" After you've answered that question, begin to implement changes.

Understanding Nonverbal Cues

Many books have been written about how to interpret "body language." Most of these books do not espouse scientifically proven information and, in fact, are deficient in accurate, reliable information.

In the persuasion process, interpretation of nonverbal cues is essential. However, there is not a "dictionary" of body movements that translate into words. To be sure, each person has certain physical movements that often can translate into attitudes and, occasionally, words. However, body movements of one person can, and often do, mean totally different things when compared to the same movement of another person.

Some body movements can send mixed messages to others. Listed below are some nonvocal cues that you should be aware of in the communication process.

1. *Hand or finger to nose or mouth*—This movement often sends the message that the speaker may be lying. In general, keep your hands away from your face and head when in the persuasion process.

2. *Feet on floor*—While communicating, keeping your feet on the floor is a neutral signal. In other situations, it is a negative signal if coming from a man.

3. *Arms crossed*—Never cross your arms when communicating because many people perceive this as a defensive signal regardless of why your arms are really crossed.

4. *Eye contact*—Maintaining eye contact is critical when responding to penetrating questions. Breaking contact once you begin to respond vocally may be perceived by your listener as lying.

5. *Walking*—When you walk by yourself into a room, you should be taking consistently moderate length strides at a moderate pace, standing erect, with hands cupped, shoulders back, and eyes ahead (not down at the floor or up at the ceiling). If you're walking too slowly, most executives will perceive that you have nowhere important to go. If you're walking too quickly, it will be perceived that you don't carry much authority in the corporate structure.

6. *Jewelry*—Simple jewelry like cufflinks, tie tack, watch, and

one or two rings are OK. As a general rule, necklaces and earrings are out for men.

7. *Briefcase*—Your briefcase should be thin. If more than two volumes of *Encyclopedia Britannica* can fit in it, it's probably too big.

One interesting note should be made here. Most people do behave similarly when trying to *control* emotions such as fear, anger, and frustration. It is relatively easy to control facial muscles at such times. Conversely, it is difficult to control finger movement, feet movement, breathing, and perspiration, especially on the palms. This phenomenon seems to be cross-cultural.

The only other movement that seems to be cross-cultural and generally recognized is the smile.

Even eye contact, a sign of honesty in America, is heavily frowned upon in many contexts in countries like Japan. Let's consider a couple of examples of how the *same* body language from two people sitting next to each other can have divergent meanings.

• Two people can be listening to a proposal and both are nodding their heads in apparent agreement. Their internal dialogue, however, can be very different.

A. "Wow, this is a wonderful opportunity. We should really go for it."

B. "Yeah, yeah, let's get this one over with. I told you I'd give you fifteen minutes and that's it. I've got a ball game to get to. No sale, buddy."

• A speaker is giving a lecture. Two people in the front row are continually readjusting their positions in their chairs. The speaker assumes they are bored. The internal dialogue is, once again, very different.

A. "Geez, this speaker is great. I wish he'd take a break; I've got to go to the bathroom."

B. "My darn hip. That doctor said it would be fine after two weeks. I've been waiting a month to hear this speaker and now I can't handle the pain. I might have to leave before he's done."

If we try to overgeneralize our interpretation of nonverbal cues, our conclusions could be very misleading indeed. It is best to read the cues in the context of each situation.

If we determine that nonverbal communication in any given instance amounts to 60-90 percent of the communication, what assumptions and generalizations can we make for the prediction of other people's thoughts and behavior?

1. *Body physiology can be a powerful clue to the state of mind of your listener.*

If you want to gain a sense of what your counterpart is feeling, assume the physiology he has. If he is standing tall, has a big happy grin on his face, and is generally animated, when you assume his physiology you will probably discover that he is enthusiastic about something. You also gain rapport, which is very valuable in the persuasion process.

Often when you present an idea or proposal to a prospect, he will be "stone-like." He doesn't move. He stares at you or your proposal and shows no other nonverbal cues. You don't need to assume this physiology. My experience has generally revealed that two things can be going on in this listener's mind.

A. "He's not going to convince me to do X no matter what he says."

B. "If I sit like a rock and stare, he'll eventually just have to leave."

Fortunately for the Master Persuader, this person will be

easily convinced of your idea, product, or service. This is a very easy wall of defense to deal with. It may not be easy to knock down, but it will be easy to *go around it!*

It is necessary to get the listener involved in the process physically. Hand him something for examination or approval. Whatever you hand him has to ensure a positive response. Once he has moved to take your offering, retract your hands and sit back while you ask questions about your product/service/proposal. Then be prepared to reveal something else that the listener can touch or read that is unquestionable in validity.

2. *Body physiology is important to the degree it changes in your communication with your counterpart.*

Two people are standing, having a nonthreatening conversation about sports. The tone of the conversation is positive. One person switches the conversation to a controversial subject like religion or politics and, at a specific point in his communication, the other sits down and folds his hands at a table while continuing to listen. Something has changed in his mind. Possibly, this is how he "prepares for battle." The reaction could also be defensive, hoping the issue will soon pass. The point to be noted is that his *state of mind has changed* from the sports conversation to the present conversation.

As mentioned earlier, you are not likely to persuade someone whose physiology you have not assumed. So in the instance above, it would be wise to sit down at the table in a conversational/cooperative proximity and assume the physiology of the other person.

Although each individual has physical movements that carry general verbal translations, remember that they don't necessarily carry over from person to person. Unless you know the person you're communicating with very well, you cannot put a label on his behavior such as "folding hands while sitting at table equals X." You do know one thing, and that is *some-*

thing changed. You can probably assume it was not for the better as far as accomplishing your persuasive objectives, so you will need to meet your counterpart once again in a physiological state similar to his.

When you become well acquainted with an individual in an ongoing relationship, you *will* be able to put "labels" or "definitions" on hand movements, postures, flinches, facial expressions, and other physiological movements and changes. When you know an individual's body language, you will interpret communication with greater precision. You can still make mistakes in interpretation, but considerably fewer.

You can learn to read effectively your close friends' and relatives' body language only by carefully watching physiology, then comparing it with what is being said by them in conversation and interpreting the context of the conversation accurately.

Congruency

Congruent means "in agreement." Your verbal and nonverbal messages should be congruent. Some of the most common congruency problems are identified below.

1. *Smiling all the time*—Smiling is important when you greet someone, solve his problem, and/or say good-bye. When you are identifying needs and values and during neutral parts of your presentation, you should be businesslike.

2. *Vocabulary and speech patterns don't match socioeconomic levels*— Your presentation should match the speaking patterns of the people who will be listening to you. Most presentations should be simple enough for a ninth grader to understand, and have a vocabulary to match. Jargon is out unless you are 100 percent comfortable with it and it fits your listeners.

3. *Losing rapport with the prospect*—As Master Persuaders, we

"mirror" or model the physiology of our prospects. This makes the prospects feel comfortable with us and builds rapport. Once we have rapport, we should never lose it due to "product knowledge overkill." Don't impress people with how much you know about your product. Keep it simple.

Once you know that your nonverbal cues are congruent with what you are saying, and you are in rapport, you can begin to get verbal agreement from your prospect with undeniably true statements.

Examples:
  "You own the store?" Yes
  "You'd like to have greater cash flow?" Yes
  "Bigger profits are always nice, aren't they?" Yes

As the prospect answers undeniably true statements, your rapport becomes more powerful and the likelihood of gaining yes answers to additional questions increases dramatically.

Once in rapport, you need to inch closer to your prospect physically. If you are sending congruent messages, this will be accepted. If not, you will need to "back off." All successful salespeople touch their prospects as discussed earlier in the book. However, coming too close too soon can burst their "comfort bubble" and kill the proposal. Monitor feedback carefully and be congruent.

Key Points Outline: The Impact of Nonverbal Communication

I. The importance of nonverbal communication

II. Proxemics
  A. Using fixed and semifixed space

B. Using informal space
C. Using touch

III. Strategic movement

IV. Physical appearance

V. Understanding nonverbal cues

VI. Congruency

PARADIGM OF PERSUASION

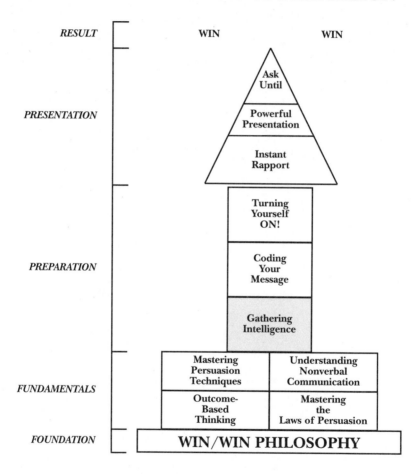

CHAPTER 6

Intelligence: How to Get It, How to Use It

Knowledge itself is power. —Francis Bacon

You can make more friends in two months by becoming interested in other people than you can in two years trying to get other people interested in you.

—Dale Carnegie

It is often noted that it is the military that first gains access to new technology and information. Only when the military, and thereby the government, has access to technology do we become aware of it. Pertinent information is called "intelligence" by the government and the military. The Master Persuader needs to gather, analyze, and utilize intelligence for a successful encounter with a WIN/WIN result as well.

Many people believe that humans all think alike. This belief is not only incorrect but risky. A 1995 study released at the University of Arizona painted a clear picture of gender differences. The research team interviewed 1,700 workers about how they would perceive a request to engage in sex by someone of the opposite sex. The results are interesting.

Fewer than 1 percent of the women were flattered.
50 percent of the women were insulted.
13 percent of the men were flattered.
8 percent of the men were insulted.

Men who believe that women operate from the same model of discussing potential sexual encounters will be greatly distressed at the responses they will get. Similarly, women will find how insignificant this notion is to men. The lesson we learn of course is to gather information before we open our mouths and start talking in relationships, business, and all other situations.

A Master Persuader gathering intelligence will seek the following information:

    1. My values.
    2. My specific needs and desires.
    3. My counterpart's values.
    4. My counterpart's specific needs and desires.
    5. My counterpart's life-style.

How can we present a WIN/WIN outcome if we don't know our own values, needs, and desires, as well as our counterpart's? We can only hope to help others with their needs once we know what those needs are.

We have determined the importance of knowing our values. These values will guide us in our lives. They will motivate us to achieve. They will drive us always to seek a WIN/WIN result. It is important to know your values and keep them in mind with every communication process.

A Master Persuader uses his skills in all areas of his life, not just in his profession. A Master Persuader is also a consumer. As a consumer, it is important that you know exactly what your needs and desires are. These should be as specific as possible. You will need to think about all the facts and figures before entering into a negotiation process.

We previously discussed the importance of determining the values of those people with whom you communicate. Learning those values with each interaction is of primary importance. It is imperative to know what drives or motivates a person in each persuasive process.

Most individuals have strategies for falling in love, buying, being happy, and, yes, being persuaded. They are not all the same. However, once you know someone's strategy, you can present your proposal to him in a way that will make it virtually impossible for him to say no. You may recall from chapter 4 that to find out a person's values, needs, and desires, we must *ask him.* Here again is how we determine the values of an individual.

Values Determination

1. "What is most important to you about X?" (e.g., buying a car, owning a house, marriage, a job, etc.).
2. "How do you know when you have X?"
3. "What's next most important to you about X?"
4. "What else is important to you about X?"

Obviously, you will not be able to use these exact words in all persuasive settings. So, you will have to adjust your questions to gain information in each different context.

The process of gathering intelligence will be different for every encounter. Every persuasive situation is different and some information may not be available to you. Some information may be irrelevant. It is up to the Master Persuader to use Outcome-Based Thinking to determine what intelligence will be necessary for each encounter.

Intelligence Gathering for the Consumer

Have you noticed that the process of purchasing a vehicle from a dealership is almost as painful as going to the dentist?

It's true. What is the latest trend in automobile marketing? "No-haggle purchasing." Because everyone pays the same price for the vehicle, you theoretically get the same deal as everyone else. This knowledge has been proven to set a customer's mind at ease. The trend will continue to grow. Look around for automobiles that fall into this category and you will be absolutely certain that the owner of the vehicle is someone who is a very poor negotiator! The vehicles themselves are probably as good as any other, but the key selling point is "no haggle—no hassle."

Even if someone pays $700 over invoice or more, he doesn't care. It was a pleasant buying experience and he gained the nice low-pressure atmosphere while paying too much for the car. The car company wins as it gets a much larger commission per unit. The individual wins as he does not have to face a great deal of stress.

In chapter 2, we analyzed the OBT process for my purchase of a new Toyota Camry. Let's use the same type of example here to show what I would do to gather intelligence for the same kind of encounter. (I don't buy "one-price-only" cars. It's too much fun the old-fashioned way!)

For the first step in this particular example, I would obtain an issue of consumer-oriented publications like *Consumers Digest* or *Consumer Reports* that dealt with purchasing new cars. I would objectively and subjectively compare the Camry to other cars in its class as far as quality and reliability. Then I would find the car's wholesale and retail costs. I would take notes on the specific model I wanted and then determine the total cost of the car with all the options desired.

Next, I would contact several banks to determine which had the best financing option available for new-car purchases. I always ask each bank to chop ¼ percent off the interest rate offered by the previous bank. Eventually I find the rock-bottom rate, which is usually about one full point below the advertised rate!

Armed with this intelligence, I would know how much I

should expect to spend, and whom I can finance it through. If the dealership wanted to finance the car, it would need to beat my best interest rate or no deal. This is not likely to happen. In any process of persuasion, it must always be a WIN/WIN result or no deal. (Remember, if you pay more when you could pay less, they win; you lose.)

It will be extremely difficult to produce a WIN/WIN situation in the persuasion process if you have not done proper intelligence work. Intelligence work is critical to your success. You are fish bait in a pool of sharks if you have not done your homework and know your numbers going in the door! Buying a car is usually the second-largest investment most people make. It's also usually the worst investment most people make!

The biggest investment most people make is the purchase of a new home. Most buyers want to begin by selecting a home, and only then considering financing, price, insurance, taxes, and the other expenses involved. Of course this is how to spend much more than you need to.

The proper way to buy a new home is to begin gathering intelligence before selecting an agent or looking at any homes.

Let's say you will be in the market to buy a new house within the next year. The first thing you would do is *learn about buying a house.* You would find out how much you would *save* per $10,000 in purchase price if you were to get a fifteen-year loan as opposed to a thirty-year loan like most people (who end up in a WIN/LOSE situation). Next, you would determine not to waste your money on anything more than a fifteen-year loan. You would call lenders in the area to determine interest rates and point fees. Be sure to ask what additional costs would be involved and find out if the *seller* could pay those fees. Learn how each lender's adjustable-rate mortgage programs work.

Next, find out what fees and costs various mortgage companies are willing to waive in order to have your business. The only way you can do this is to have a list of *all* closing costs from each mortgage company. The way you get that is by calling the company, talking to a loan officer, and asking for an itemized list of all costs.

Next we need to determine worst-case scenarios that assume interest rates will skyrocket and never come down. We do this in case we decide to get an adjustable rate or two-step type of mortgage. (It's very unlikely that interests will go up and stay up for fifteen to thirty years but it is always wise to calculate the worst case that can happen!)

Our next step is to determine how much you could afford to pay monthly for principal, interest, taxes, and insurance, and add in extra for utilities and upkeep.

If possible, you will undoubtedly want to drive through the different parts of town and decide what areas you'd like to live in. If you have children, stop in and visit the schools nearby.

Now, you are closer to being ready to contact a real-estate agent. Most real-estate agents will tell you that they work at 7 percent commission. Unfortunately you can't pay that because you are not wealthy. You offer 4 percent and the guarantee to give full commission to the agent when you sell your house. Some companies have a floor they will not go under, usually 6 percent. If you are unhappy with the floor that the company set, feel free to find a new agent or company. It is also possible you may find a hardworking agent to whom you are willing to pay 6 percent. That of course is fine. Money is not the only commodity of value in the world.

Once you have found an agent and a home that you are interested in, you would have it inspected by a professional. Every flaw would need to be fixed before purchase.

To detail everything in the gathering of intelligence in just this area would be unfeasible. I'm sure you see, though, that there is much to do before you will even begin to look at houses!

Each time you go to the store and make a purchase, you in effect are helping to shape public opinion. If you purchase Product X, when it is scanned at the checkout counter, it is immediately noted for reorder. Had you chosen Product Y instead, you would have created a reorder for Product Y. The reason why this is important is that every purchase is a net win for one company and a net loss for every other competing company. When enough of Product Y is moving versus Product X, it will get more shelf space, closer to eye level than product Y. Go into the grocery store and see which cereal is at eye level and which is on the floor and you will know where the money is being made.

Once the company who makes Product Y has been fortunate enough to get you to buy its product, it wants to know more about you. It wants to know where you fit in, demographically speaking, and it wants to get you personally to buy its product(s) again. In order to gain this information, companies often attach special offers to a product, where you can send in a coupon and get a special deal on some other product, usually related. When you send in your order, they now know who you are, where you live, what your approximate income is (based upon the neighborhood you live in), and any other information you filled in on the coupon. This information is entered into a database with all the other people who replied by mail and now the company knows the demographics of who is buying its Product Y.

Product Y is not done with you yet, though. Now the company will do two things with you. First, if the company is wise, it will put a "cents off" coupon in with the product so as soon as you are out of the product you can go buy another one and have a coupon in hand. You probably don't have a Product X coupon so you will have an incentive to purchase Product Y again if you liked it equally or more than Product X.

Secondly, the company will direct mail you on occasion. Because you have responded by mail once it will continue to seek information from you in the future. You may receive a long survey with more questions about demographics. You may not even recognize that the survey is from the company that produces Product Y. It may "farm out" the survey to a marketing company who will ask you to compare Product Y with Products X, Z, A, and B. Then it will want to know which is the best and why. Once the company has this information it can market more effectively to meet your values, needs, and desires. It can also upgrade its product if the public demands it.

There is much more that will occur each time your name and address get on someone's "list." It's not necessary to go into detail here about all the aspects of marketing. It is fascinating to consider how a company can manipulate its database to market more effectively and produce better products. Because of the more precise information the company gleans from you, it can now for less money persuade you to purchase its products. In this particular instance the consumer and the company both WIN!

Data is manipulated daily to the detriment of the average person in America. Privacy is becoming a thing of the past. Virtually anyone in the world can get a credit report that lists all your debts, how quickly you pay them (or don't), and much more information related to your daily life. The federal government knows so much about you that if you knew what it knew, you'd be incredibly upset! (The government can find out whom you donate money to, whom you work for, how many children you have, how old they are, what you spend your money on, and so on. Consider everything that you send in with your tax forms every year.) Clearly, the data available on you and me is there and can be used against us, and it often is.

Cultic Intelligence

Many cults, which we will speak of as groups of people who try to break away from society for religious, political, or philosophical reasons, abuse the data that is given to them by their members. (*Note:* Not all "cults" are bad. There are often very positive reasons for creating communal living and separatism. Here we simply provide an example of how a cult could, as some do, abuse the information given to it by its members.

The same pattern can be seen in many corporations and even family situations, as you will gather. . . .)

Disgruntled with your current church for whatever reason, you search for the truth elsewhere. You become convinced that a certain group has some answers to questions that you had not heard of before. You believe that by following the doctrines of this new organization, you will be more closely aligned with the wishes of your Creator. (*Note:* How you got to this point is a completely *different* discussion as it relates to persuasion, which will be dealt with later in this book.)

"Knowing" that this group is closer to the "truth" than anything you have seen before, you become more dedicated to the certainty of its doctrines. When you first were in touch with this group, you told them of your frustrations with your current church, shared many beliefs, possibly confessed to many sins, etc. All this can be recorded easily after discussions with the group's leader or other people in the church. Soon a number of people have access to your sins, your past, your background. They know where you are weakest and are capable of exploiting that knowledge.

First, a group can exploit this with the threat of the loss of salvation or the good graces of the Creator should you leave. This of course can be backed up with several Scriptures from the Bible when taken out of context. Fearing the *pain* of Hell or darkness and the possible loss of the rich experience of *pleasure* of Heaven is often enough to keep even the most stubborn or awakened person in a cult. The thought of "what if they are right?" goes through your mind. The threat of *great pain* is often subtle. It matters little as long as the person is convinced. For many it stops thoughts of leaving. For others, though, it does not.

For those who determine they wish to leave the group regardless of the spiritual threats of damnation, there are threats of a disconnection from all the friends made in the group. Once again with various Scriptures taken out of context it is easy to show the person that she will not be able to see any of her friends anymore. The friends will all know that some evil has overtaken the person wanting to leave. They will be brokenhearted, but they will know where their highest value is.

The leader, minister, or someone else in the group will gently but firmly explain that by leaving you will be all alone. (The need for bonding is often one of the greatest reasons for joining *any* organization, not only a cult.) No longer is the pleasure of salvation the strategy to keep the member involved. Now the group is using pressure with "fear of loss" (pain) on a very tangible scale. Where the leader *could* be right that you will lose out on salvation (or whatever benefit comes from being in the cult) by leaving, now he can state with certainty that you *will lose* all your friends.

If this works at this point and you remain, all is well in a manner of speaking. If not, and you are still determined to leave, it is possible that *more* than persuasive or coercive tactics will be used. Violence or the threat of violence for leaving a closed society is often possible. Many cases occur every year in the United States alone. This implied threat of violence goes past the spiritual and emotional to the physical. Now the threat is striking at one's most basic self. Physical punishment is something few can tolerate. Although it is still possible the person will leave the group, the fact is that it will be very difficult to do and may cause the individual great distress for the rest of her life.

It's clear that this is a case where the individual loses. It is very sad, but there are small groups and large countries where this is true.

Can you think of any countries (before or since the cold war ended) that killed or tried to kill "traitors" or those wishing to leave? Can you think of organizations or groups that can use excommunication as a form of keeping the group "pure"? Can you think of groups that tell members that their beliefs or doctrines are the *only true* beliefs and doctrines?

You already know that writing down seven answers to each of these questions is a great idea and will help you remember this *very* important abuse of the powers of persuasion!

Meet John Doe

What if you are dealing with more than one person, or a small group of people? What if you are a salesperson and see hundreds of people per year? What if you are a direct-mail marketer and your written documents will reach thousands of people? Is there any general information about people that is valuable in the process of persuasion?

On any given day, the average person in a free market society is absolutely bombarded with persuasive messages. The average person has some of these perceptions:

1. "There are so many different kinds of widgets, I don't know which one I should buy." For a person with this perception, your message will want both to create the need for John Doe to buy your widgets and, in simple terms, explain why your widgets are better than your competitor's widgets. If they aren't better, you need to give John a solid emotional reason to do business with you. (Example: "Tylenol, the brand doctors recommend most.")

2. "I wish I knew more about widgets. It scares me to buy any. What if I make a mistake?" Your message in this case needs to address his fear of making a bad decision. (Example: "Alka Seltzer: try it, you'll like it. Ahhh.")

3. "The neighbors have these widgets. I should have some, too!" Your message here should impress upon John that many people own your widgets and love them. People in his community have been using your widgets for years. Look

how much better life is for them! (Example: "Pepsi: the choice of a new generation.")

4. "I feel kind of guilty buying widgets when I should be using my money for other things." Your message in this case should give John confidence that it's OK to go ahead and buy some widgets. He works hard all week and really *deserves* them. You want it? Go for it! You'll be glad you did. (Example: "You asked for it, you got it: Toyota.")

5. "I feel kind of crummy about myself. Haven't been too happy lately. I wouldn't enjoy widgets even if I had them." Your message here will have to paint a picture of John as excited, prosperous, happy, confident, attractive! (Example: "Wouldn't it be great if . . . you were the photographer of the swimsuit issue? Wouldn't it be great if you had a Keystone beer?")

In general, people aren't as happy as they could be. Most people only have a moderate amount of self-esteem. Two-thirds of all women and one-third of all men don't like the way they look in a mirror. Nearly everyone worries and has a deep-seated fear of rejection. We are also afraid to grow old, die, and, of course, be in pain. We don't really know how much products cost or even how much they are worth. We have little time for being smart shoppers and don't comparison shop much. When we get our mind set on something, we want it *now*. Credit cards are still plastic and aren't real money. We want to make decisions that will make us look good. We are a lot like John Doe!

Realizing this is who John Doe is, how do we sell to him and market to him? How do we make use of the information used by the largest advertising firms worldwide?

Among the very best research on how to advertise products and services successfully is *Ogilvy on Advertising*. Author David Ogilvy was called "the most sought-after wizard in the advertising business." His book stresses the importance of intelligence in advertising. He recommends objective research as well as subjective communication with product buyers.

Once we know what our prospects' needs, wants, and values are, we can use this information to prepare a message that firmly impresses upon the prospects' minds how we can help them.

If we were to isolate one model of successful advertising, this would be a good one:

1. What you presently have, who you presently are, or how you presently feel is not satisfactory. *You can do, have, or be more* and *feel better.*

2. Product/service X helps *many people just like you* get that result.

3. Try it once. You have nothing to lose *and everything to gain.*

4. *Other people will respect you and like you more* for using this product/service.

5. *Imagine* your future as you deserve it to be. You can *reach your dreams* and achieve your goals if you use this product/service.

6. This product/service is *guaranteed* so you can feel *secure* in making a decision *now.*

Obviously, not all market messages use this model or all parts of it. But, based on the intelligence of researchers worldwide, this model appeals to John Doe.

Research shows that John Doe *does* act *now* when responding to this model! How can you implement this model in your sales or management career?

This advertising model, combined with the following research information, will give you the intelligence you need to plan a powerful presentation that will take into account the life-style of your prospect or counterpart and project a WIN/WIN outcome for both of you.

A group of researchers chose to break down Americans into five marketable groups. The groups were categorized according to values and life-styles.

1. *The Belonger* (37 percent of Americans)

Values and Life-style: Family, hardworking and proud of it, hate change. Traditional American: 71 percent of all belongers live in the Midwest; 66 percent are blue-collar workers. They buy Coke, Budweiser, and shop at Kmart and Wal-Mart. They go to traditional churches and don't like new ideas. They drive American cars, eat at McDonald's, and use AT&T.

2. *The Emulator* (20 percent of Americans)

Values and Life-style: Aged nineteen to thirty-nine. Seek material success. They want to succeed and value confidence. They believe that if they have enough confidence, they will become successful. Many times, the reason why they want success is so they can enter into sexual relationships. Emulators have a powerful sex drive. The top 5 percent of emulators are yuppies. Those in this group are probably overextended on credit cards. They often cannot pay for the life-style they live. They drive new cars or old BMWs. Emulators buy more clothes than any other group, wear Levi's, drink Dr. Pepper or Michelob, and use Sprint or MCI. They want to be wealthy and that is often their driving force.

3. *The Achiever* (18 percent of Americans)

Values and Life-style: Earn $70,000+ and have absolute

confidence. The achiever's number-one value is to be unique. He will do anything to keep from being one of the pack. He doesn't like to waste time. Achievers drink Heineken and buy only the best, high-quality products. They are mostly Republicans. They have no sympathy for the lazy and inept.

4. *The Societally Conscientious* (22 percent of Americans)
Values and Life-style: Environmentally conscious, love outdoors. Afraid of being manipulated, don't trust others. Subgroup A: Grew up in 1960s and haven't changed and adapted to today's culture. Subgroup B: Cut their hair, adapted to the system, and are turning it around. The societally conscientious are mission oriented. They may have negative associations with money. They are the most highly educated people in world. There are more college graduates in this category than in all others combined. Their average age is forty-one; they tend to buy Volvos or Subarus and eat Grape Nuts. They don't like hype or high pressure. They shop at wholesale clubs and co-ops.

5. *The Need Driven* (3 percent of Americans)
Values and Life-style: Survive by government assistance, welfare, or are retired. They buy one-dollar-per-month insurance policies and are generally elderly.

How do you use this data?
Find out which category you best fit. Each time you meet someone, determine into which category he would fall. Being aware of the general group into which people fall provides a fairly good basis for predicting their specific values, beliefs, and life-styles. This data does not ask you to put people in "boxes." Use the information combined with the model for John Doe presented above to plan your presentation.
In the early 1990s a "new" VALS (values, attitudes, and life-styles study) was done and the categories were altered a bit.

The results were very similar to those listed above, but as time marches on, the number of need-driven Americans is growing larger and larger. With the federal government going deeper and deeper into debt and the percentage of elderly people increasing, this will become a very large segment of the population by the early 2010s and the 2020s.

The area of the population it will most likely draw from will be the belonger category. The notion of "buying American" will become less important to more people with fewer global restrictions. As the world becomes "smaller" in the sense of communications, people's loyalties will expand globally. Environmentalism will go head to head with capitalistic entreprenuers.

By knowing the general "category" a person falls into, you can then predict his values with more efficiency. This is the core of marketing, sales, and, of course, persuasion.

Putting a Strategy Together

Returning to the subject of ethical persuasion, we are now ready to prepare our message. The example below shows how we might determine a person's life-style and use the information for a successful WIN/WIN close. It will also present a basic game plan for persuading this individual. We will use a sales situation as our setting. The Master Persuader is an advertising-space salesman. The prospect is a restaurant owner. The meeting place is the prospect's restaurant.

Name: John Williams
Title: Restaurant owner

Life-style category: Belonger
Why: Very hardworking restaurant owner, puts in seventy to eighty hours per week. He emphasized on the phone the fact that he has certain advertisements he likes to stick with.

Laws to be used:
Law of Contrast
Law of Association
Law of Consistency

Techniques to be used:
Clarity of Values
Use of the Name
Future Pacing

Advertising points to stress: 1. What you presently have, who you presently are, or how you presently feel is not satisfactory. *You can do, have, or be more* and *feel better.* 2. Product/service X helps *many people just like you* get that result. 3. Try it once. You have nothing to lose *and everything to gain.* 4. This product/service is *guaranteed* so you can feel *secure* in making a decision *now.*

Intelligence: The salesman would like Mr. Williams to purchase an advertisement in his newspaper, the bigger the better. But he doesn't want Mr. Williams to overextend himself if business isn't that great. The salesman will want the owner to be able to pay for his ad! It seems that Mr. Williams keeps his restaurant extremely clean and runs it efficiently. His business has been in the neighborhood for twenty years, according to the owner of the video shop next door. When the salesman stopped in Wednesday, about ten employees were working. Menu prices were standard. Mr. Williams advertises heavily in coupon books, co-op mailings, and local papers. About two-thirds of the seating was filled on Wednesday night. There must be *lines* on Friday night! Mr. Williams has never been asked to advertise in this brand-new local paper before.

Strategy: The salesman should be sure to get Mr. Williams to sit down for the meeting. He should comment on the cleanliness of the restaurant, and call him by his first name. He should also comment that Mr. Williams must put in lots of hours keeping the place running so smoothly and efficiently. Then, he should ask questions to clarify the needs of the restaurant and Mr. Williams in particular. The salesman should focus on new customers, people in the community who know he's there but don't go out much. Since the restaurant owner, as a belonger, will most likely be hard to convince that a change will be worthwhile, the salesman will want to stress the ad point #3—try it once. You have nothing to lose, *and everything to gain*. Also, he'll want to mention names of other restaurant owners who have done similar advertisements. Show him the half-page ad in *contrast* to the quarter-page ad. Have a layout ready to show the owner when he walks in the door. The salesman will need to conduct himself just like the owner, brief and confident. Ask the owner if profitability is important to him. Show *profitability*. The salesman should mention a money-back guarantee if the ad does not produce satisfactorily.

In the above example, the intelligence is brief. The more significant the communication is to be, the more information you will want. In each situation, you will determine which laws of persuasion you will utilize and which techniques of persuasion you will need. The salesman will have testimonials, a general planned presentation, and a general closing offer already prepared that he uses six to ten times daily.

Gathering intelligence is critical to producing WIN/WIN results in the persuasion process. The more you know about an individual or group, the more you will be able to tailor your communication to their specific needs.

Instead of viewing the gathering of intelligence as time-consuming work, look at it as detective work with you searching for clues. You are solving the mystery of what makes another human being "tick." Learning about other people can be very exciting. Finding out what makes people "tick" is one of the rewards of the communication process.

This kind of intelligence gathering is fairly generic in nature. Now that we live in the information age, businesses, churches, political organizations, nonprofit organizations and just about any corporate entity have the ability not only to gather but store and manipulate data quickly and efficiently. As is the case with everything else detailed in this book, the knowledge can be turned into power for great good or for control, prejudice, and evil.

Key Points Outline: Intelligence

I. Intelligence in the persuasion process
    A. Values determination
    B. Intelligence gathering for the consumer
    C. Cultic intelligence

II. Meet John Doe

III. Advertising model
    A. What you presently have, who you presently are, or how you presently feel is not satisfactory. *You can do, have, or be more* and *feel better.*
    B. Product/service X helps *many people just like you* get that result.
    C. Try it once. You have nothing to lose *and everything to gain.*
    D. *Other people will respect you and like you more* for using this product/service.
    E. *Imagine* your future as you deserve it to be. You can *reach your dreams* and achieve your goals if you use this product/service.
    F. This product/service is *guaranteed* so you can feel *secure* in making a decision *now.*

IV. Life-style categories
    A. The Belonger
    B. The Emulator

PARADIGM OF PERSUASION

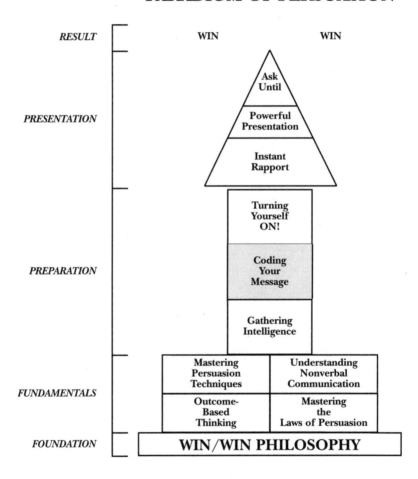

CHAPTER 7

Communication Styles: Preparing the Message

Men must be taught as if you taught them not, and things unknown proposed as things forgot. —Alexander Pope

How often misused words generate misleading thoughts.
—Herbert Spencer

The previous chapter of this book is very intense. After all, gathering intelligence can be the most challenging aspect of the persuasion process to many individuals. However, this chapter is fun! We will take a break from laws and techniques and turn on the channels of communication. In preparing the message, we must remember that we are attempting to persuade *people*. This chapter will introduce you to the different communication styles used by people and how to code our messages so that they are accepted by our listeners.

We know how to set our objectives, use Outcome-Based Thinking and the laws of persuasion, and apply various techniques, verbal and nonverbal. We know how to find values, ours and our counterpart's, and use intelligence in the persuasion process.

Yet, while we know all of this and more, we can still fail miserably in attempting to persuade others if we don't code the message in the listener's general communication style.

137

It would be impossible to give the Meyer-Briggs personality test to everyone we want to persuade. (The Meyer-Briggs test helps people learn more about their personality.) We *can* understand a person's basic communication style very quickly after engaging him in a short conversation. Once we know that style, or channel, we can code our messages to work on that channel. People appreciate this, even when they are unaware you are doing it! This will become crystal clear as we continue.

Consider two factors when determining a person's basic communication style. First, determine whether a person is a mostly logical or a mostly emotional person and, second, whether a person is a mostly assertive (extroverted) or a mostly nonassertive (introverted) person. Use the chart below for reference.

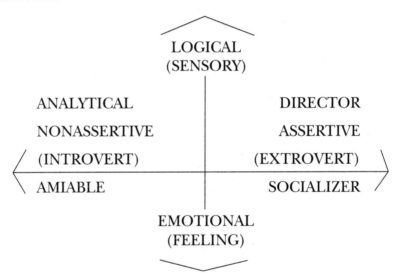

Psychologist Carl Jung developed the theory of categorizing personality types in the 1920s. His work will serve as the basis for our understanding communication styles. For our purposes, we will use the most basic and simple classifications of personality styles. People with different personalities communicate differently.

Some of the characteristics of the various styles appear below. Determine which category best fits you.

Analytical

Logical, Sensory, Nonassertive, Introvert

The Analytical is a slower-paced individual who is a consistent, steady, methodical worker. The Analytical is well prepared and is often good with numbers, analyses, processes, and systems. The Analytical is often a perfectionist. He enjoys problem solving and in-depth conversations. Working alone is how most Analyticals prefer to do their tasks. Analyticals follow directions and rules. The Analytical is a diplomat and normally doesn't hurt others' feelings. On the other hand, the Analytical is often short on giving praise!

Some famous Analytical characters would include Sgt. Joe Friday of "Dragnet," Mr. Spock of "Star Trek," and Data of "Star Trek: The Next Generation."

Analytical people make good accountants, auditors, bookkeepers—positions where you need someone to get a job done quietly and calmly. Don't expect them to be the life of the party. They will be on time, though.

In the persuasion process, you have your work cut out for you with an Analytical. Analyticals *don't* make decisions from instinct. In fact, they tend to be skeptical from the start. You will need evidence, proof, facts, details, complete explanation, and as much documentation as you can muster. Analyticals, of course, need time to "think about it" and can't be pressured into making a decision *now!*

Director

Logical, Sensory, Assertive, Extrovert

The Director is *fast* paced and task oriented. Directors are in charge and want results at all costs. Directors don't waste time and know things get done when they are in control. Most Directors are very self-confident, independent, and strong willed. They like a challenge, take charge in unfamiliar situations, and decide quickly. Directors are impatient and expect everyone to work as hard as they do. Directors tend to be contrarians more so than other personality types. Directors enjoy being dominant by creating their own world. They want their accomplishments noted.

Famous directors include Capt. Jean-Luc Picard of "Star Trek: The Next Generation," ex-Chicago Bears coach Mike Ditka, General Patton, Lou Grant of "The Mary Tyler Moore Show," and Colonel Potter of "M*A*S*H."

Most Directors think quickly, so they often make decisions with whatever facts are available to them at this moment. Director's make good CEOs and excellent entrepreneurs; they tend to excel in any position where they are in charge. The Director will throw a good party, expect people to be on time, and note those who aren't. Directors often have a rough edge to them. They are interested in results.

Directors are easier to persuade than most personality styles. They make decisions quickly if you can present your proposal quickly, effectively, and convincingly. Be prepared to speak more quickly and get to the point more rapidly than you normally would. Directors should be "closed" in a sales situation with an "alternate choice" close such as, "Would you rather have it in red or blue?" Tell them what your product does or what your idea is, do it quickly, and tell them what the outcome of their decision will mean for them. Be brief. Hit the key points and leave the details for the Analytical who balances his budget.

Socializer

Emotional, Feeling, Assertive, Extrovert

The Socializer is the one who loves being the center of

attention. Socializers are fast paced, enjoy being in relationships, and like being with people. Socializers love entertaining and being entertained. They love to have fun. Socializers tend to exaggerate and generalize. They are talkative, spur-of-the-moment types. They tend to be enthusiastic, friendly, and optimistic. They tend to go with their intuition.

Famous Socializers include most entertainers: Jay Leno, Joan Rivers, Oprah Winfrey, Geraldo Rivera, and Phil Donahue (notice the connection), Rhoda of "The Mary Tyler Moore Show," Hawkeye, Trapper, and B.J. of "M*A*S*H."

Socializers throw a great party, but are not good with details. At an extreme they are sometimes flighty and seem to be going in all directions. They can talk on the phone all day. Socializers make good receptionists, hair stylists, customer-service people, etc. Many socializers become entrepreneurs but generally don't do as well as Directors because they are more emotionally oriented.

To persuade the Socializer is not difficult at all, but it time consuming. Socializers have little concept of time! Socializers need to know that the proposal you are presenting to them would be accepted if you offered it to other members of their group. You'll need to constantly acknowledge their self-worth. They need recognition. If you can use the law of conformity, and show them who else uses your product, the Socializer can be easily persuaded to your way of thinking. Keep your presentation exciting, upbeat, and enthusiastic—no boring facts and figures.

Amiable

Emotional, Feeling, Nonassertive, Introvert

Just about everyone loves an Amiable. They never make waves. If a Director is a series of powerful ocean waves, an Amiable is a still pond. They are relaxed, casual, and love relationships. They are very feeling-oriented people. They wouldn't think of hurting your feelings and wouldn't believe it if you were to hurt their feelings. Amiables, unlike Directors, are happy with the status quo. There is seldom reason for change. Amiables are great listeners, agreeable, supportive, and good counselors. They seldom take risks in any way. Amiables have a hard time saying no. (They also have a hard time saying yes!) Amiables are slow to make decisions and don't like arguments or fights. They are kind, patient, and considerate. Other characteristics would include warmth, friendliness, loyalty, and dependability.

Famous Amiable characters would include Counselor Troi of "Star Trek: The Next Generation," Laura Petrie of "The Dick Van Dyke Show," Bob Newhart on "The Bob Newhart Show," Woody of "Cheers," and Radar O'Reily of "M*A*S*H."

Persuading an Amiable is an interesting process. If you come on as aggressive, excitable, or too enthusiastic, you will probably repel him. Gentle is a key word here. The Amiable needs constant reassurance that he is making a good decision. You will need to build rapport and appear to be in the process of forging an important relationship before he will be convinced of your sincerity. The Amiable has to "feel right" before any kind of decision can be made.

Once you know what "category" fits you best, you can more objectively perceive others' communication styles. Consider each style of communication as one of four alternatives, neither inferior nor superior to your own. Your job in the persuasion process is to learn to adapt to each communication style and code your message so that it will be acceptable to your counterpart.

It will take time to become unconsciously competent in this new skill. As we learn who people are and how they communicate, we learn what they are most likely to respond to, both positively and negatively. We enter into their communication channel.

Imagine an Amiable person trying to persuade a Director.

The Director would become very frustrated over the Amiable's need for a relationship and his slow pace of speaking. The Socializer would go nuts when presented at length with an Analytical's numbers and figures.

Exercise: Take one sheet of paper and write a dialogue between two people. The scene is an Amiable car salesman selling a Director prospect. On another sheet of paper, write the dialogue for an Analytical man asking a Socializer woman out on a date. What conversation ensues on the date?

I'm sure you noticed that these people communicate in different ways. Let's consider one way to break down the communication-style barriers and build some bridges.

For years, top executives and salespeople have known that one way to work with other people effectively in the persuasion process is to match and mirror other people's behaviors. This helps the communication process in an important way. It creates a comfortable setting. Matching and mirroring also works well in interpersonal relationships.

Since the 1970s, a technology called Neuro-Linguistic Programming (NLP) has become valuable for studying communication. NLP is the study of the structure of subjective experience. It gives us a model of how people think and how people represent their perceptions and communications within the mind. It sounds complicated, and some of it will be dealt with in part 2 of this book. Here we can touch on some of the more readily understood and applicable components of NLP.

Essentially, NLP allows you to do anything better than you already do it.

NLP allows us to build bridges between people for effective interpersonal communication as well as in the persuasion process. Our purpose at this point is simply to present those models and techniques that apply to the persuasion process. In part 2 of this book we will learn some more sophisticated models and strategies of NLP and hypnosis, and how they relate to the persuasion process.

Everyone represents events in their minds in different ways.

There are three general categories of representational systems. These are Visual, Auditory, and Kinesthetic (feeling). Some people's dominant (most important) system is Visual; for some it's Auditory; for others it's Kinesthetic. Everyone will use each of these systems, but most people have a definite preference.

Based upon communication styles covered earlier in this chapter, would you guess the Amiable to represent things in the mind as feelings, or pictures? If you said feelings, you'd be right in most cases. People who speak slowly, tend to ponder, and get a feel for things, are broadly speaking, kinesthetic in nature. They almost always fit in the Amiable communication style.

What about the Director? The Analytical? The Socializer? Let's examine each representational system and learn how to build bridges between you and each of these other types of people.

Visual

People who represent things in their minds with pictures, more so than sounds or feelings, are termed Visual. Visual people speak rapidly as pictures flash through their minds. They *tend* to be Directors or Socializers. They like to look at pictures, diagrams, charts, videos, and graphs. Their gestures are very quick and angular. They use words like "see," "view," "light," "imagine," "picture," and "look." Their breathing tends to be high in the chest, shallow, and quick. These characteristics will make it easy to identify the person who represents visually in his mind.

The best way to deal with a visually oriented person is to increase your speaking rate to match his and use the same type of words he does. Use pictures, diagrams, charts, and other audiovisual helps.

Auditory

People who represent things in their minds with the spoken word are termed Auditory. Auditory people speak moderately and rhythmically. They tend to use words like "click," "hear," "tone," "sounds good," "listen," "in tune," and so on. Their breathing is midchest and rhythmic.

In order to persuade an auditory person (who can fall into all four communication styles), you must moderate your vocal rate, breathe deeply, and use words that fall into the auditory linguistic patterns. "That sounds right, doesn't it?"

Kinesthetic

People who represent things in their minds with feelings and sensations are termed Kinesthetic, or feeling in nature. Kinesthetic people look down a great deal. They speak slowly. Their breathing is deep and slow. They use words like "feel," "touch," "grasp," "hold," and "contact." Kinesthetic people tend to fall into the Amiable communication style. Sometimes, you will find a Kinesthetic person who falls into the Analytical category.

The best way to persuade a Kinesthetic person is to slow down. Breathe deeply and relax. Be calm in your communication. Use words that will make a Kinesthetic person feel comfortable.

Later, in part 2 of this book, we will learn more about representational systems and how to use them in a far more powerful way.

Remember, as you plan your communication, plan it so that you are on the same communication channel as the listener. Make certain you use language that will appeal to the listener and speak at a rate consistent with your prospect's.

Now think of seven people you know well. What category do they most fit into of the personality types? Write down *why* you think so. Think of seven favorite people you know. They can be relatives or friends. What communication style/personality type do they fall into for the most part? Are they the same as yours? The opposite of yours? What category do most of them fall into? Which of these four styles of communication are you mostly in? What style do you best communicate with?

Encoding our messages for other people means we always have to be conscious of how the people around us like to communicate. If we want people to enjoy our presence we must operate in their channel of communication. It really is a simple matter to speed up our speaking process when talking with a Director or Socializer and slow down when dealing with an Analytical or Amiable. Making use of words that appeal to each of the three representational systems at first may seem clumsy but after a while it becomes second nature.

Up until now, we've primarily dealt with external communication. The next chapter will focus on internal communication. It's time to turn yourself on!

Key Points Outline: Communication Styles

I. Determining communication styles
    A. Analytical
    B. Director
    C. Socializer
    D. Amiable

II. Neuro-Linguistic Programming
    A. Visual
    B. Auditory
    C. Kinesthetic

PARADIGM OF PERSUASION

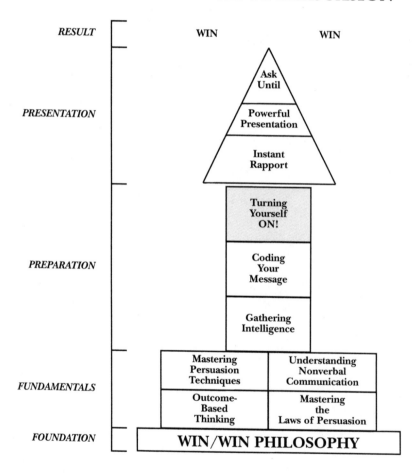

CHAPTER 8

The Power Within You: How to Achieve Mastery of Yourself and Power with Other People

The value of life lies not in the length of days, but in the use you make of them; he has lived for a long time who has little lived. Whether you have lived enough depends not on the number of your years, but on your will.

—Montaigne

The unexamined life is not worth living. —Socrates

Action springs out of what we fundamentally desire.
—Prof. Harry A. Overstreet
Influencing Human Behavior

Many people enter into the persuasion process with only the knowledge and tools we have dealt with in the first seven chapters. (This would put you in the top 5 percent of communication experts if you have mastered the content of the book to this point!)

In this chapter, you will learn how to transform yourself into a successful and dynamic communicator. You will learn how the most charismatic people in the world are able to command devoted followers. You will learn how to have a powerful influence over all those with whom you come in contact.

149

The Master Persuader knows how to use all the laws and techniques we have studied. The Master Persuader is an expert in using nonverbal communication, proxemics, intelligence, and word power. The Master Persuader also has the key ingredients that ignite these tools into Total Power. These ingredients make up *mastery of the self.*

The Six Keys to Mastery of the Self

Few people in this world are true masters of themselves. Earlier, the importance of goals and values was shown to be essential to the persuasion process. Now we must make the quantum leap toward mastery of the self.

1. Passion

What is it that motivates you? What do you want out of life? What do you feel compelled to do for others in this lifetime?

Those individuals who feel obsessed with providing value for others and for themselves have powerful motivation. Being obsessed with getting the most from life that you can get will allow you to reach states of mind you've never reached before.

Passionate people are, without a doubt, the most effective persuaders on Earth. When you believe so strongly and love with such a fervor that which you are convinced of, your complete mental dynamics work with a supercharged power. When other people are near the passionate person, they know that there is something special about that person and respond in exciting ways.

Can passionate people be quiet? Absolutely! Passion is a state and has many different manifestations in human behavior. A passionate person is not always talking. Can you think of times when a passionate person may not be talking at all?

Passionate people are often described as having "charisma." Charisma is supercharged personal magnetism that draws devotion from throngs. Charisma has always seemed to be an intangible quality that some people have and others do not. This is simply untrue.

People like Elvis Presley, Michael Jackson, Martin Luther King, John F. Kennedy, and Marilyn Monroe all possess(ed) this powerful charisma. They all had in common the ability to enter a state of passion at will.

We must become passionate if we are to persuade others.

Become passionate by being in love with life and others. Be excited that you are alive when others more deserving are not. Focus on those things that compel you to reach your dreams. Look forward, realizing that yesterday is not tomorrow. It is gone and only something we can learn from. Tomorrow dawns bright and we can be bold in facing it. Life holds adventure and incredible challenges for those who dare to walk in the unknown.

When you focus on your dreams and what you will be doing daily to attain them, you will begin to burn inside with a new lust for life. People will want to be around you as you become like a personal magnet.

As a person with passion, you will attract good things and people into your life. This is the first ingredient of self-mastery. If passion is the flame, then faith is the spark.

2. Faith

As you move toward your dreams, they become like a sunrise. First you see only the top rim of the sun. Soon, the huge ball will ascend high into the morning sky.

How do you know that? Because it always has!

When you know you can accomplish something, you are willing to set out and do it. Like the sunrise, you simply know you will accomplish your goals.

The Bible is a book of faith. Among the wisdom on the subject of faith in the Bible, two golden nuggets are worthy of note:

"Faith is the . . . confidence of things not seen."

"Faith without works is dead."

When a carpenter is preparing to build a house, the house exists only in his mind. Other people do not see the house, yet he is confident it will be there. However, if he simply sits on the lot where the house is to be built and "wishes" it were there, it will never come into reality. Faith without work(s) is dead!

Earl Nightingale, the world-famous twentieth-century success philosopher, said that "Thoughts are Things." Late in the twentieth century, neurosurgeons proved his statement true. When you can picture something precisely and in detail in your mind, you can bring it into reality. As noted above, it will take *confidence and work.*

People with great faith also have powerful persuasive abilities. The Apostle Paul nearly single-handedly brought the Christian faith to the pagan people of the Roman Empire. To be sure, he had help, but it was he who was instrumental in the spread and growth of Christianity. His mission spread the gospel to all the world. He believed he could do it, pictured in his mind that nothing could stop him, went out, took action, worked hard, and changed the world with the message of Jesus of Nazareth.

When you have great faith, you have another ingredient in self-mastery. People of great faith are powerful persuaders. Paul was a Master Persuader.

3. Rapport

Noting the incredible persuasion powers of the Apostle Paul brings to mind one of the great persuasive speeches ever made. In the seventeenth chapter of the book of Acts, you will read the words of a Master Persuader. Notice how Paul uses rapport to prepare his listeners.

The setting is this: Paul is in Athens, Greece. Athens has a pagan culture. The city is filled with idols and temples to mythological gods. This is repugnant to Paul as a Jew and a Jewish Christian. Some of the local philosophers have challenged Paul to a debate. They bring him to Mars Hill.

> Men of Athens, I perceive that in all things you are very religious. [This gets their attention. Giving a compliment is an excellent way to start a persuasive speech.]
>
> . . . for as I was passing through and considering the objects of your worship, I even found an altar with this inscription: TO THE UNKNOWN GOD. Therefore, the One whom you worship without knowing, Him I proclaim to you. [He uses the persuasive laws beautifully. The altar is one of *their* objects of worship. The God he wants to discuss is one of *their* gods. He is not going to talk about some new god!]
>
> God, who made the world and everything in it, since He is the Lord of the heaven and earth, does not dwell in temples made with hands. [God *made* the world, he tells them. He's *obviously* much too *big* to live in a human temple!]

Paul continues his discourse, explaining that God gives us life, breath, and a place to live. He explains that God needs nothing from us.

> . . . for in Him we live and move and have our being, as also some of your own poets have said, "For we are also His offspring."
>
> Therefore, since we are offspring of God, we ought not to think that the Divine Nature is like gold or silver or stone, something shaped by art and man's devising.

Paul points to the Greek poets as his authority. He makes it clear that, as God's offspring, we should not think that God is like stone or anything man could make!

> Truly, these times of *ignorance* God overlooked, but *now*

commands all men everywhere to repent, because He has appointed a day on which He will judge the world in righteousness by the man He has ordained. He has given assurance of this to all by raising Him from the dead.

Of course, at this juncture, the choice was clear. Many mocked Paul. Many others joined him and believed.

The rapport Paul gained with the antagonistic philosophers is the key here. He did not begin by informing the Greeks that they were fools to be worshipping idols made of stone. No indeed! He complimented them on their obvious religious attitudes.

After gaining rapport, he used the laws of persuasion very effectively as he quoted Greek philosophers (and poets) and finally used a step-by-step, logical approach to an emotionally charged issue. Had he *not* gained rapport at the outset, he would have lost the entire audience. Instead, he polarized no one, and used documentation and argumentation methods that they were familiar with. Paul was a Master Persuader. One wonders if he had any inkling of what long-term changes his work would make over the entire earth!

Of course, building rapport involves more than complimenting those you wish to persuade. Rapport goes much farther than the verbal aspect of communication. Rapport shows understanding and interest. It shows a true concern.

As we have seen, rapport is the key to gaining the trust and confidence of others. If people have rapport with us, we can easily ask them to agree with us. Rapport creates affinity.

Rapport is a nonverbal linking of two or more people. Once you are able to achieve this, you will have the evidence of true self-mastery. Only after we have mastered ourselves can we become truly excellent in the persuasion process. We will consider the various aspects of nonverbal communication as they relate to self-mastery, rapport, and the persuasion process.

a. *Physical Appearance*—An individual's dress and grooming will greatly affect whether others perceive him as likable or not likable. A long-haired young man in jeans and a T-shirt will not likely gain rapport with an older man in a business suit. The Master Persuader dresses and grooms to create affinity with those he wants to persuade or gain devotion from.

b. *Vocal Cues*—As discussed earlier in the communication styles, it is best to gain rapport with others by speaking at the same rate as them and using the same specialized vocabulary.

c. *Posture*—The quickest way to gain rapport is to use your physiology the same way your counterpart does. You will want to sit or stand exactly like your counterpart. This is called *pacing*. You can check to see if you are in rapport a minute or two later by adjusting your body posture and seeing if your counterpart follows suit. If the listener does adjust to your new posture, you most likely are in rapport and the listener will be very open to your proposals.

d. *Breathing*—Breathing is very important in building rapport. The Master Persuader will always model the breathing of his listener.

The objective of rapport is to send a subconscious message to your counterpart that you are just like him. When you are just like someone, you are likely to gain that person's trust. Your proposals will gain credibility and you will be perceived as having integrity. When people trust you, all "defenses" come down and your listeners will be completely open to your proposals and the persuasion process.

4. Outcome-Based Thinking

People with great charisma and, of course, the Master Persuader have made OBT part of their mental makeup. They know where they are going, why they are going there, and they consistently get themselves back on track as they are driven off course by the events in daily life.

The Master Persuader uses OBT in all facets of his life. Not only are his dreams holographically visualized and the plans laid for reaching his vision, he also has predetermined the outcome of his conversations in daily life. When someone tries to take him off course, he lovingly and politely brings the conversation back on course toward the predetermined outcome.

Outcome-Based Thinking is not a technique. OBT is a way of life. The charismatic individual is always prepared for a situation that could go awry because the charismatic always has contingency plans. This is why most charismatics are Master Persuaders. They know what they want, why, and how to get back on course.

A critical skill of OBT is the ability to reframe any situation that comes up to your own benefit. Look at these examples and then we will analyze them. (*MP* denotes Master Persuader.)

PROSPECT: We can't afford life insurance. We just don't have the money.

MP: John, *that is exactly why* you need it. What would happen if you died tomorrow? Isn't it worth it to protect your wife and son?

HUSBAND: I don't want to paint the house this summer. It's just too hot.

MP: *That's exactly why we should.* You know as well as I do, a coat of paint will help insulate the house and save us money in air conditioning this summer and heating this winter. You do want to save the money, don't you?

HUSBAND: I don't want to go out tonight. I'm too tired.

MP: *That's why we should.* You need to get out and enjoy

yourself. You work too hard. Let's go out, have fun, and get your juices flowing again.

PROSPECT: I don't think we can quite afford this car.

MP: *That's exactly why you should* buy it. You've seen the repair records on this car. Nothing ever goes wrong. The used car you are driving will be costing you hundreds to thousands of dollars a year in upkeep *plus* your payment. For the same amount of money, wouldn't you rather be driving the new '97?

PROSPECT: I'd like to donate to your cause, but I've never heard of it before.

MP: *That's exactly why you should donate now.* You yourself said you believe in what is being done by us to help young children. With the support of people like you, the cause will gain recognition rapidly and next year when I come back, you'll be happy that you went ahead and helped out.

OBT is a completely new way of thinking for most people. Once a predetermined outcome has been set, the subconscious does everything in its power to get you there.

Does that sound real? It should. How many times have you driven to work in a daze, and you literally do not remember having driven there, yet you arrive safe and sound at the front door?

The next time someone gives you an excuse that something shouldn't be done, think of why *that's exactly why he should* do it!

It will take repetition, practice, and conscious effort to develop OBT. As you can see, the work will prove fruitful!

5. Personal Power

Personal power is the ability to take action. You may have heard the wisdom: *"The road to hell is paved with good intentions."* Intentions may be nice, but action provides results. If you want to be a charismatic Master Persuader, you must use your personal power. You can have the previous keys to self-mastery, but without the ability to take action, you won't see your desired outcomes.

Personal power is 100 percent within our control. Is our true desire to enter into WIN/WIN relationships, or will we continue to enter into LOSE/WIN or LOSE/LOSE relationships?

Not using your personal power is like getting ready to take a vacation but staying home. The car is packed, the family is buckled up, the key is in the ignition, the car is started and *the driver does not shift into gear and go!* Until you *go,* you are, at best, getting ready! No one has fun getting ready!

As you use OBT, and know the results you want, please *go and get them!* You cannot be a Master Persuader if you give up at the first sign of resistance. You must persist until you succeed in obtaining your predetermined results.

Procrastination is like practicing for death. When you visualize the results you want, make the results so enticing that you *must* go and get them! *Do it now!*

6. Power with Other People

People gravitate toward passionate individuals. Passionate individuals tend to be consistent in their thoughts, and, as has already been detailed, consistent people are trusted. Trusted people are believed.

People who have passion for life, ideas, products, services, and beliefs will be much more effective in persuading others to their point of view than will dispassionate people. People who have the ability to attract a vision for others to see or believe have devoted throngs.

You can have the same results as people of passion if you will become passionate about your life, beliefs, ideas, products, and services. You can have power with other people if you will become totally focused on helping others reach their goals and attain their highest values. You can have power with people if you are always pursuing a WIN/WIN situation in the persuasion process.

Ultimately, you can have power with other people to the extent that you have mastery over yourself.

At this point, you are just about ready to enter into the persuasion process. It's time to turn you on!

Before you enter into the persuasion process, regardless of whether you will be influencing your spouse, your boss, your team, or a crowd of listeners, you need to be in a powerful state of mind. You must be unstoppable!

Future Vision

Read these instructions through once, then follow them.

Close your eyes and remember a time when you were totally self-confident, a time when you knew you could achieve what you wanted and then you did. View the experience from the vantage point of how you experienced it. *You* should not be in the mental movie. *You* should be reliving this experience. What kinds of things were you saying to yourself? How did you feel? What behavior allowed you to achieve what you wanted? Memorize these things! Relive this event and relish the intensity in your mind. Take your time.

Now, take all these feelings, sounds, and images that make you feel confident and powerful and imagine the person or group you are going to persuade. Feeling the same confident, powerful feelings, persuade the person or people to your way of thinking right up to the point where you achieve your goal in the process. Take your time. Relish those positive feelings. Enjoy your success.

Now, open your eyes, and find how confident and powerful you feel.

There is nothing mystical about this procedure. The reason it works is very simple. The brain cannot tell the difference between a "real life" experience and one that is vividly imagined using all the senses. When you remember an experience, the brain is literally reliving it.

Additionally, you have the opportunity to *create* memories. Regardless of how good or bad your past was, you can add to your memories by imagining your *future!* You can literally help create a more powerful you, using your imagination.

The power of the imagination should not be underestimated. None of the remarkable technologies we have in the twentieth century would have been possible if they had not existed in someone's mind *first.*

Thoughts are things. Everything is created twice. Everything is created in the mind and *then* in reality for the rest of the world!

Therefore, if you want to use your mind to its fullest extent, for greatest success in the persuasion process, you must get all you can out of it.

Picture the problems at hand and solve them quickly in your mind. Picture in your mind those individuals you must persuade, enter into the process, and allow the listeners to accept your proposal.

If you are a salesperson and are in a slump, go through ten or twenty presentations in your mind and have all your prospects buy from you. You'll find your sales slump is very short-lived. Your brain will tell you that business is great and will allow you to get "on a roll." Have you ever been on a roll when everything went your way? You can create these feelings all over again to become unstoppable.

Self-talk

"Don't think of your car."
"Don't think of ocean waves."
"Don't think of President Clinton."

What did you think of? Your car, ocean waves, and President Clinton. As we discussed earlier in this book, the brain has been programmed since birth to have a tendency to override the word "don't."

Look at the statements again. By eliminating the word "don't" (cover it with your finger), the brain did exactly what it was told to do. Now consider the following:

"Don't be so stupid."

"Don't act like a jerk."

"Don't get into trouble."

You're way ahead of me. You know that these statements are commanding the brain to do exactly these actions.

The things we say powerfully affect others as well as ourselves. These examples of bad self-talk illustrate negative hypnotic language patterns and should be avoided always. Even "off the cuff" remarks about ourselves or others can be very positive or very negative. So, we must be extremely careful.

After visualizing full-color, bright, up-close "movies" of positive outcomes, we can work on the second most powerful tool for instant power: self-talk.

Self-talk needs four elements to effectively help you achieve powerful states of mind.

1. Self-talk must be stated in positive terms.
2. Self-talk must be stated in the present tense.
3. Self-talk must be powerfully stated (with emotion).
4. Self-talk must be precisely stated (so you can prove what you're saying)!

Self-talk should always be stated positively. What do you think the following statement is really telling your brain?

"I won't get fat."

If you said, ". . . get fat," you're right! Instead, say, "I look great in the mirror today wearing size-34 pants again!"

"But," you say, "I wear 38s! Who am I kidding?"

You aren't kidding anyone. Your brain believes that you

wear 38s. Your brain will say "liar" when you first use your self-talk. After a while it will say, "Huh, I guess he does wear 34s," and will allow you to lose the weight to squeeze back into 34s.

"I am confident and calm in the persuasion process. I achieve the objectives I set for myself and have created a WIN/WIN situation."

This is self-talk stated in the positive. More specifically, let's assume a woman wants her husband to take her out tonight. She would use self-talk like this: "John will enjoy taking me out tonight. He will find me appealing to be with and will want to go out much more in the future because of the fun we will have tonight."

A car salesman would use self-talk like this: "It's funny how things have changed. At the rate I'm going, I'll sell twenty-five cars this month. People seem to have rapport with me immediately and can't say anything but yes when I ask them for a commitment."

Every day, you have roughly sixteen hours of mental stimulus and eight hours of sleep. The eight hours of sleep we shall disregard as far as this book is concerned. If you have fifteen hours and fifty-nine minutes of negative stimulus from yourself and others, do you really believe that one minute of positive self-talk will change your life?

Positive self-talk, like Outcome-Based Thinking, has to become a part of your way of life. We have all been programmed so poorly for years that we need to get to work right *now* with positive self-talk.

Brian Tracy, one of America's most intelligent speakers, says we should repeat short phrases like "I like myself," "I'm the best," etc. Plugging these thoughts in our minds minute after minute is like putting nickels into an empty piggy bank. At first, it isn't much, but it soon grows and grows.

W. Clement Stone, author of *Success System That Never Fails*, uses the phrase *do it now* as his self-starter. "Do it now" is one of the most powerful phrases you can use. When in doubt, "do it now!"

The confidence and power you will add to your self-concept through self-talk will greatly enhance your likelihood of success in persuasion. Because positive self-talk is a "subset" of Outcome-Based Thinking, it is good training for the mind. Within twenty-one days, you will notice the benefits of self-talk if you will use it consciously on a daily basis.

You can write your own self-talk. Remember, it must be *positive*, stated in the *present tense* ("I am . . ." is an excellent start for self-talk scripting), *powerfully stated*, and *precise*.

Allowing yourself positive self-talk will give you another advantage. It will cause you to be focused on positive thoughts. This will help to prevent you from experiencing negative emotions like fear and doubt. Use the power of focus as an ally in all your communications.

If at any time you begin to experience fear or negative emotions while in the persuasion process, you are thinking about the fear instead of objectively listening to the speaker's point of view. Even if what the speaker has to say makes you nervous, you can still eliminate your negative reactions by trying to "get inside" the speaker's mind and focus on *why* he is saying the things he is.

Proper Physiology

We've used the techniques of future vision and positive self-talk for instant power. These techniques link to our visual and auditory representational systems. Before entering into the persuasion process, we also would be wise to use our physiology properly.

Stand as you would if you were feeling totally confident that you were going to succeed in your persuasion process. Breathe deeply and slowly in through the nose and exhale slowly through the mouth. Do this three or four times before entering the room where you will be communicating.

While standing tall, taking those deep breaths, remember

the pictures you had in your mind when you were totally confident and feel how it felt.

Think of people who are very powerful in their demeanor. What is their physiology like? How do they stand and sit when they are in a powerful state? Think of people who are very weak in some way. What is their physiology like? How do they stand and sit when they are in a "weak" or "feeble" state? Think of someone who recently was very depressed and when you told him some exciting news he perked right up. Write down all of these thoughts with the rest of your notes you have been keeping. It is by doing these simple exercises that you will recall this information quickly and be able to use it without making a conscious effort.

Key Points Outline: The Power Within You

I. The six keys to mastery of the self
    A. Passion
    B. Faith
    C. Rapport
        1. Physical appearance
        2. Vocal cues
        3. Posture
        4. Breathing
    D. Outcome-Based Thinking
    E. Personal power
    F. Power with other people

II. Future vision

III. Self-talk
    A. Stated in positive terms
    B. Stated in present tense

C. Powerfully stated
D. Precisely stated

IV. Proper physiology

PARADIGM OF PERSUASION

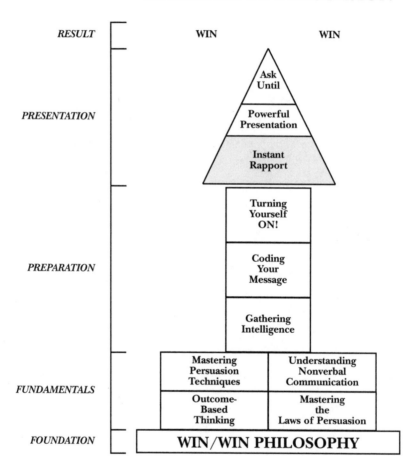

RESULT   WIN   WIN

Ask Until

PRESENTATION   **Powerful Presentation**

Instant Rapport

Turning Yourself ON!

PREPARATION   **Coding Your Message**

Gathering Intelligence

    Mastering Persuasion Techniques   **Understanding Nonverbal Communication**

FUNDAMENTALS   **Outcome-Based Thinking**   **Mastering the Laws of Persuasion**

FOUNDATION   **WIN/WIN PHILOSOPHY**

CHAPTER 9

Instant Rapport

Many people fail to make a favorable impression because they don't listen attentively.   —Isaac F. Marcosson

Take the tone of the company you are in.
                                        —Earl of Chesterfield

First, arouse in the other person an eager want. He who can do this has the whole world with him. He who cannot walks a lonely way.   —Prof. Harry A. Overstreet

The ability to gain the respect, trust, and liking of a stranger during the beginning stages of the persuasion process marks the skill of Instant Rapport. In the first stages of communication, or of your presentation if you are a speaker or salesperson, you will need to gain rapport, discover values and lifestyles, and identify needs.

When a person is unable to generate rapport with someone else, then no relationship of any significance can take place. Rapport is essential to persuasion and to all communication.

Imagine that it is the dead of winter and a car is stranded on the road. The person's battery is dead. You come along, park in front of the other car, and hook up the jumper cables. Positive goes to positive and negative goes to negative. You get in your car and rev the engine. He gets in his car, turns the key, and lo and behold the car starts right up. You are a life-saver and the person is very grateful.

Now imagine that same cold winter night and the same person stranded. You hook up the cables but you get them backwards. You accidentally hook positive to negative and negative to positive. You get in your car and rev your engine. The stranded motorist turns the key in his car and the battery *explodes!* Assuming no injury to the poor man, you now have some serious problems on your hands. A good intention has turned into a disaster.

In each of these tales, the jumper cables are metaphorical for the proper or improper use of rapport. Rapport can be mechanical like the jumper cables or it can be a true spiritual and emotional affinity for another person. When we start communicating with someone, we have an opportunity to build rapport. When this is properly done, we end up with a grateful person on the other end of our communication. That is our goal. If we do not build rapport, we attach the jumper cables backward and explode the communication process and possibly the entire relationship.

Our objective in the persuasion process is to help the other person understand as closely as possible what we are thinking. There is always a lot of interference in trying to communicate an idea to someone but the process can be effectively accomplished *if* we have built rapport.

For example, you like someone and are interested in furthering your relationship with her. You are thinking of your cute little poodle and you are going to ask the person if she likes dogs. This poodle is very important to you and you don't know if you could get along with someone who didn't like your poodle.

"Say, Anna, do you like dogs?"

Anna gets a sudden shiver down her spine. She was bitten by a huge German shepherd when she was a child and she just recalled the whole event all over again.

"No, I try to keep away from them at all costs!"

Now, if two individuals truly care about each other, if they have good rapport, then they will sort through this kind of confusion. What has happened here is that both people had different versions of reality as to what a dog is. One person thinks a dog is a cute little poodle and the other thinks a dog is a German shepherd.

If the two individuals are not in rapport with each other then they will not continue the discussion. Due to this single communication failure, a potentially gratifying relationship has been missed.

Had the rapport been strong, then something like this may have occurred:

"How can you not like cute little poodles?"

"Poodles?"

"I mean, I've never met anyone who wanted to keep as far away from poodles."

"Poodles? I thought you meant *big* dogs like German shepherds."

"Huh? No, I have a poodle named Tinkerbell. She is so cute. That's what I was asking."

"Poodles are OK by me. I was talking about, well, you know . . . "

Now, of course, you do know! You should have asked if she liked poodles and she should have asked what kind of dogs. The degree of rapport between you two is what will determine which scenario gets played out. It is just this reason why rapport is so critical in the communication and persuasion process. (Precision is critical as well and we will discuss greater precision in the persuasion process later in the book.) The greater the rapport or affinity between two people the greater the chance of any communication problems being worked out to the benefit of both individuals.

The more people think alike, the more they like each other. The more similar people's pictures are in the communication process, the closer they are to each other spiritually, emotionally, and physically.

Let's return to a scenario introduced in chapter 6: the advertising-space salesman and the restaurant owner. We have already done the Intelligence work and have discovered the preparatory information. We will now study the dialogue as a Master Persuader gains rapport and gives his presentation.

The salesperson, Ken Harding, enters the restaurant wearing suit and tie. He carries a thin presentation folder in his left hand. He looks around and notes that the restaurant is very slow for this afternoon. Slow business means the owner will most likely not be able to afford advertising and *that's exactly why he should* be buying. Ken's newspaper has an excellent track record for its positive advertising results. The place is very clean and quiet. The owner of the restaurant, John Williams, is completing ringing up an order at the cash register. He says good-bye to a customer. Ken approaches the cash register and says nothing.

JOHN: May I help you? [Moderate rate and volume: possibly Auditory in nature.]

KEN: John?

JOHN: That's me.

KEN: Ken Harding with the *Gazette*. I spoke to you Friday on the phone. You told me I should stop by at two o'clock today to inform you about a special promotion the *Gazette* has prepared for restaurant sponsors. I'll only need about seven minutes of your time. Can we sit down? [Points to a corner booth. Ken says he will only take up seven minutes because he is aware that John's communication style is Director. Also, the precision of "seven minutes" promotes credibility and trust.)

JOHN: I see. [This indicates that John is probably Visual too.] Right this way.

KEN: How long have you had the place, John? [Note use of the name.]

JOHN: This will be our sixth year. [Still a moderate speaking rate.]

KEN: How is it you guys are able to do all right in a recession when so many others are not doing so well? You must put in lots of hours here." [Ken notes this fact because he has determined that John is a belonger. John provides beverages for each of them. Ken is sitting facing the cash register. John sits facing Ken, unable to see anything but Ken. *Note:* Use of proxemics.]

JOHN: Oh, I don't know if we're doing that great. We've got our regulars and that keeps us goin'. [He fingers his straw and stirs his pop.]

KEN: [Fingers his straw, stirs his water, and takes a sip, modeling John.] "I don't know, John. I talk to a lot of businesspeople and it seems like some guys know how to bring people in. What kind of advertising or promotions have you found that pay off?" [Ken asks a question to determine John's values and needs.]

JOHN: It's hard to tell if you don't run a coupon, and if you do run a coupon, you're paying to give your regulars a discount and lose twice.

KEN: Is there anything that's worked, that's been profitable?

JOHN: [Leans forward.] Well, we run a half-price dinner with the purchase of a full-price dinner in the direct-mail program. That does pretty well for us.

KEN: [Leans forward, also.] How do you decide if you've done well enough to do something again?

JOHN: Well, we've got to make money on it, or we can't do it.

KEN: If you were to make money with a promotion in the *Gazette,* would you run it again in the future? (Ken asks this question to make use of the law of consistency and the technique of future pacing.)

JOHN: Sure, if it made money.

Sold!

Most salespeople never get this far, and if they do, they have no idea what to do next. We know that John Williams is sold at this point because he has stated that he would run this kind of ad in the future if it were profitable for him. This implies that he will run it now, so that he can determine if it will be profitable for him. The future-pacing technique has been successful for Ken.

Next, all Ken will need to do is work out the details. He may run into some objections from John before he can actually close the sale, but if Ken can keep in mind the intelligence he has gathered, that should not be a problem. He still has many options available to him from his presentation strategy. In the process of closing, Ken would be wise to (1) mention some other restaurant owners who have used this ad successfully; (2) stress that the ad space is guaranteed to be profitable, or he will get his money back; (3) use the law of contrast to give John two options to choose from for the size of the ad to purchase; (4) all the while, stay in rapport with John, speaking at the same rate and using words that will appeal to his Auditory and Visual representation systems; and (5) keep in mind that John is a Director personality, so won't need *all* the facts and figures Ken may have available. John will want only the bottom-line facts.

Consider what is necessary for establishing rapport, discovering values, and identifying needs.

The Seven Keys to Instant Rapport

1. *The Master Persuader models the prospect*—A large part of gaining rapport with others involves mirroring physiology including posture, gestures, movement, and breathing. Vocal cues and words are also important.

2. *The Master Persuader shows sincere interest in the prospect*—If a salesperson isn't truly interested or doesn't want to become truly interested in others, he has selected the wrong profession. It's hard to use sincerity as a technique. You are either interested in other people, want to be interested, or simply don't care. Either way, the prospect can tell.

3. *The Master Persuader confirms he's in rapport with the prospect*—He can do this by shifting his body posture in an effort to "lead" the prospect to do the same thing. If the prospect follows his lead, they are in rapport. If the prospect does not, the salesperson will need to return to mirroring or "pacing" the prospect.

4. *The Master Persuader asks questions to discover values*—Start by asking, "What's most important to you in . . .
    A. life?"
    B. a relationship?"
    C. buying a house?"
    D. making an investment?"

E. accepting a proposal?"

F. buying products or services?"

5. *The Master Persuader asks questions to discover rules that define values*—Start by asking, "How do you know when you have . . . ?"

A. Prospect responds to the question 4A above, "What's most important to you in *life?*" with "happiness." MP then asks, "How do you know when you have happiness?" Prospect may respond, "When people tell me I'm a good person."

B. Prospect responds to the question 4B, "What's most important to you in a *relationship?*" with "trust." MP then asks, "How do you know when you have trust?" Prospect may respond, "When my friend tells me everything."

C. Prospect responds to the question 4C, "What's most important to you in *buying a house?*" with "it has to be a good value for the money." MP then asks, "How do you know when you have a good value for the money?" Prospect may respond, "When I pay less than the appraised value of the house and I get the best possible deal."

D. Prospect responds to the question 4D, "What's most important to you in *making an investment?*" with "it has to be totally safe." MP then asks, "How do you know when you have a totally safe investment?" Prospect may respond, "When I can't lose anything."

E. Use the models above to create anticipated responses to your proposal, products, or services.

6. *The Master Persuader asks questions to identify needs*—Start by asking, "What is it, exactly, that you need from . . .

A. life?"

B. relationships?"

C. a house?"

D. an investment program?"

E. my proposal?"

F. my products or services?"

7. *The Master Persuader asks questions to discover rules that define*

needs—Start by asking, "How do you know when you have . . . ?"

A. Prospect responds to the question 6A above, "What is it, exactly, that you need from *life?*" with "success." MP then asks, "How do you know when you have success?" Prospect may respond, "I'm making enough money to have investments on the side."

B. Prospect responds to the question 6B, "What is it, exactly, that you need from *relationships?*" with "a balance of give and take." MP then asks, "How do you know when you have a balance of give and take?" Prospect may respond, "I'm not always just listening or complaining."

C. Prospect responds to the question 6C, "What is it, exactly, that you need from *a house?*" with "large enough for my whole family." MP then asks, "How do you know when you have a house large enough for your whole family?" Prospect may respond, "It's got to have eight bedrooms and room for a dog."

D. Prospect responds to the question 6D, "What is it, exactly, that you need from *an investment program?*" with "I need a flexible program." MP then asks, "How do you know when you have a flexible program?" Prospect may respond, "When I want to switch to a different fund, I can."

E. Use the models above to create anticipated responses to your proposal, products, or services.

As discussed in previous chapters, these questions not only give you valuable information about the prospect, they also show the prospect that you are concerned about *him* and not just your commission. In most cases, the prospect will tell you *exactly* what he needs. What better way to gain the information you need to fulfill his needs?

Modeling Emotions

Rapport goes farther than modeling physiology. It also entails modeling emotions. Emotional outbursts can impede the persuasion process. Obviously, if someone is exuberant, you will not be sitting like a bump on a log. You will be mirroring that physiology. Negative emotions are the ones that present a difficulty.

If the prospect is in an angry state of mind, and it is *not* because of something you did, you should slowly, calmly, and quietly ask, "Is there something I can help with? I sense that you are a little distracted by something?"

If the prospect decides to confide in you, you can model his emotional state but *not* his words. You should never pass judgment on someone else's anger. Eventually, of course, you will *lead* the prospect to a more positive frame of mind after he has thoroughly expressed his feelings.

In the process of building rapport with people experiencing negative emotions, never play the "one-upmanship" game:

PROSPECT: I'm so ticked off with my employees. What a bunch of idiots.

POOR PERSUADER: Yeah, I manage people, too. You think you've got idiots working for you, you should deal with the dummies I have.

This tells the prospect, "You have nothing to gripe about." What will this do for building rapport? *No sale.*

When modeling others' negative emotions, never take on as much anger or frustration as they are feeling. How could you possibly be as angry as they are? At the same time, you must validate the anger. Allow the prospect to see you *empathizing* with him.

Discovering Values

Let's look more closely at the fourth key to Instant Rapport. It is in the beginning stages of the persuasion process that you will discover values. Remember, as stated above, to discover values, you will need to ask questions.

"What is most important to you in software?"

"What is most important to you in a company that supplies you? What next?"

As professionals, we must solve problems and fill needs. Once we discover our counterpart's values, it is our job to use that information to benefit both for a WIN/WIN outcome. Let's consider how professionals discover values, solve problems, and fill needs.

Example 1

MP: Obviously, we offer numerous plans to meet individual needs. Maybe you can help me. *What do you want in an insurance policy?*

PROSPECT: We want the cheapest possible price and it has to be term insurance.

MP: *How did you decide you wanted term insurance?*

PROSPECT: We *read* in a financial book that whole-life insurance is a waste of money, but you should have term insurance. So, that's what we're *looking* for.

MP: I *see.* Aside from low cost, *what else do you want to see in a policy?*

PROSPECT: That's pretty much it.

MP: *What dollar amount do you want your wife to have in case of your death?*

PROSPECT: I was thinking $100,000.

MP: *Would that pay off your home?*

PROSPECT: Not quite. We'd need $50,000 more.

MP: OK, we should pay off your home. *Would you want your children's education paid for as well?*

PROSPECT: I suppose.

MP: *How much should our company pay for future educational expenses?*

PROSPECT: Say, $50,000.

MP: *Would you want your wife's annual living expenses covered?*

PROSPECT: Never thought of that. Yeah, I guess so.

MP: *Would you want to cover five years or ten years, or more?*

PROSPECT: Geez, how about five years.

MP: *How much should we pay for that?*

PROSPECT: Probably $20,000 per year.

MP: *Are there any other expenses we should consider?*

PROSPECT: I think that's plenty!

MP: All right, you'll have a benefit of $300,000 and, according to my chart, that works out to be $100 per month. [Looks at Mrs. Johnson.] "Well, Mrs. Johnson, *how does it feel now that your husband's protected you with over a quarter of a million dollars if he dies?*"

MRS. JOHNSON: Feels pretty nice.

This is a typical situation where the salesperson normally loses the sale early. The average salesperson goes in to tell all about the great service the customer will get and how much money the company has and how big the company is. However, the Master Persuader asks the prospect what his values are and what his needs are, then meets those values and needs. The closing question to the prospect's wife is very powerful.

The prospect is a Director, of course. He knows exactly what he wants and decides quickly. We also know he tends to be Visual in orientation. In this case, we did not have to determine other values or needs. This is often the case in dealing with Director personalities.

Example 2

MP: I want to thank you for choosing Johnson Realty. You will find that we will be very valuable in your search for a home. *What exactly do you want in a home?*

PROSPECT: We're looking for a nice, three-bedroom home with a two-car garage, in good condition.

MP: *What else do you want in a home?*

PROSPECT: Hm. Well, we can only afford so much. Maybe $100,000, or $125,000. Nice neighborhood, a fireplace would be nice. So would central air.

MP: Of all the items you mentioned, and maybe some you haven't, *what is most important to you in buying a home?*

PROSPECT: Well, it has to be three bedrooms or more or we can't take it.

MP: Sounds *very* important. *You have children?*

PROSPECT: Yes, three.

MP: OK. We need at least three bedrooms. *What is the next most important thing in buying a home?*

PROSPECT: Well, we can't afford more than $1,200 a month in payments, so that is pretty important.

MP: OK. We'll look for $1,200 a month. I'm curious—when you bought your last house, *what were the deciding factors in your mind?*

PROSPECT: Well, we were renting at the time and knew it was a lot smarter to own than rent, so we looked and found a house.

MP: *What was it about the house you eventually bought that made you decide on it?*

PROSPECT: It felt right. You know what I mean. You just get that feeling sometimes.

MP: How do you feel about the home now?

PROSPECT: We love it. It's like an old friend. But it has only two bedrooms and we've got to have the three.

MP: *What is it, exactly, that feels best about your home?*

PROSPECT: Oh, I think it's our yard. We've really put a lot of time into our garden and I guess that's one of the nice things about owning a home.

MP: Well, I believe I have enough information to get started. *Did you have anything else I need to know about or any questions for me?*

In this scenario, we had an opportunity to gain a little more information. We were able to isolate specific needs and values. We also know the individuals have certain criteria that have to be met, but the final decision will be based on a feeling. No sale is made here. This is a "fact finding" interview for needs and values.

Example 3

A recently married husband and wife are trying to decide on where to go on vacation.

HUSBAND: *What do you want in a vacation?*

WIFE: Hm. To get away from all the hustle and bustle. To get out from under all the housework and just relax.

HUSBAND: *What's the perfect place to go for a vacation?*

WIFE: Oh, I don't know. I've never given it that much thought. I used to just go with a few friends and go camping.

HUSBAND: *What exactly did you like about camping?*

WIFE: Well, I guess I liked being out in the fresh air, sitting by a campfire, and just talking. *What about you, honey? What did you have in mind?*

HUSBAND: Well, I wanted to go to Las Vegas for a week and play some cards, see some shows, and have a good time.

WIFE: Hm. I've never been to Vegas. I don't know that I'd like it much. Seems like you're leaving the rat race to get to a bigger rat race.

HUSBAND: I know exactly how you feel. I used to think that way until I went and was surprised at how fun it really is.

WIFE: I guess I'd really like to avoid all the problems of city life on a vacation.

HUSBAND: Well, maybe we can compromise. *Would you be willing to do that?*

WIFE: Well, sure, I suppose.

HUSBAND: What if we went somewhere where the air is fresh and clean, the pine trees smell beautiful, there aren't a lot of people, and I can still have fun, too. *How would that be?*

WIFE: Well, sounds good to me. Where would we go?

HUSBAND: Lake Tahoe.

WIFE: I've never been there. I don't know if I'd like it.

HUSBAND: Remember when you used to go camping with your friends and sit around the campfire and smell the fresh air?

WIFE: Yeah.

HUSBAND: Can you imagine doing that with thousands of beautiful pine trees and snowcapped mountains in the background?

WIFE: Yeah.

HUSBAND: That's Lake Tahoe. Honey, let's go to Tahoe, get away from it all, and relax.

WIFE: OK. Let's go.

In this scenario, the husband identifies a particular situation in which the wife would feel comfortable. He knows she is a Kinesthetic and, therefore, uses the word "feel." He asks the right questions to discover the wife's values and needs.

Modeling Values and Beliefs

When the people you are trying to persuade have specific values and beliefs that are important to the process, it is vital that you model or pace those points. Look at this statement:

PROSPECT: All salesmen are alike: out for the money. I don't trust any of them.

Obviously, you can't agree with the prospect. But you must appreciate the prospect's belief and acknowledge that he has the right to believe it.

MP: Sounds like you've been taken advantage of. What happened?

When you avoid the trap of fighting with your prospect, you both benefit. The prospect will have an opportunity to vent his feelings in a manner you can deal with. You have listened to his beliefs and have not discounted them, as most salespeople would.

Your job as a Master Persuader is to acknowledge your prospect's point of view and, if you are absolutely unable to agree with it, at least be determined to state that if you were the prospect, you'd feel the same way.

If the prospect is under the impression that you do not agree with his values and beliefs, you are *very unlikely* to reach a WIN/WIN agreement. Jesus of Nazareth once stated, "Agree with your adversary quickly." These words of wisdom are golden even unto today!

Identifying Needs

In previous chapters, we've discussed how to discover values. As shown above, identifying needs is done in much the same way. For example, someone who sells computer-software-related products will need to know:

1. Who will be using the software?
2. What will you be needing the software for?
3. What kind of hardware will it be used on?
4. What computer experience do the users have?
5. Does the software need to be user friendly?
6. Do you want the most or least expensive?

The only way you can identify needs is by asking questions. Don't be shy. A doctor asks all the questions he needs, and does all the examinations necessary before making a diagnosis and writing a prescription. A sales professional, and, indeed, all Master Persuaders, must do the same.

For you to gain complete rapport with another person, that person has got to feel as though you are both on the same "channel." This entails not only modeling the prospect, but identifying and modeling his emotions, values, and beliefs.

You now realize that having an understanding of nonverbal communication and being able to utilize questions to elicit needs and values is a precious skill. The power of rapport and the true affinity we have for other people make us effective communicators and able proceed to the next level of the persuasion process.

Key Points Outline: Instant Rapport

I. The seven keys to Instant Rapport
    A. The Master Persuader models the prospect.
    B. The Master Persuader shows sincere interest in the prospect.

C. The Master Persuader confirms he's in rapport with the prospect.

D. The Master Persuader asks questions to discover values.

E. The Master Persuader asks questions to discover rules that define the values.

F. The Master Persuader asks questions to identify needs.

G. The Master Persuader asks questions to discover rules that define needs.

II. Modeling emotions

III. Discovering values

IV. Modeling values and beliefs

V. Identifying needs

PARADIGM OF PERSUASION

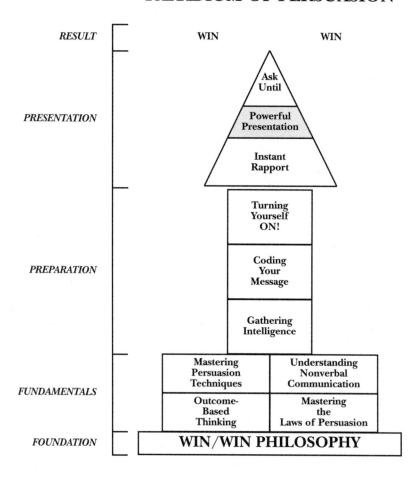

CHAPTER 10

Powerful Presentations Made Easy

Be wiser than other people, if you can; but do not tell them so.   —Lord Chesterfield

The deepest urge in human nature is the desire to be important.   —Prof. John Dewey

The people you are in communication with have come to like you at this point of the persuasion process. You know their needs and have discovered their values. Now, it is time to solve their problems and fill their needs. Presenting your ideas, services, or products is a very simple process providing you have discovered the needs and values of the person or people you are with.

Gaining rapport with your prospect is critical if you want him to accept your proposal. Now, in your presentation, you will simply fill his needs with the idea, product, or service that will most benefit him. There is an axiom that says, "No one cares how much you know until he knows how much you care."

Unquestionably, this is true. The purpose of this book is to help you persuade people to your way of thinking. You cannot achieve this goal if people perceive you as uncaring. Your knowledge is irrelevant to them if you are seen as selfish or self-serving.

Consider a very simple scenario. A woman is going to propose to her Director husband that they should have a quiet night out. He'd rather be doing paperwork, she presumes. She's got her game plan. Now she's ready for the proposal.

WIFE: [Enters den. Her husband is at the computer.] I'm glad you're getting caught up on your paperwork. If you finish it now there'll be time for other projects later.

HUSBAND: Mm hm. [Typing away.]

WIFE: I was thinking about us going away for the weekend, but I think that would be *a waste of time*. At the same time I know *you're more productive when you're not stressed out*. Would a movie help recharge your batteries, or would a quiet dinner be better?

HUSBAND: I do feel stressed out. Heck of a day. If I had five employees combined that did as much work as I do in a day, we'd double our business.

WIFE: Dinner or movie. *You pick.*

HUSBAND: Dinner.

WIFE: You want to make the reservations, or would you rather work and I'll set it up?

HUSBAND: You do it. Let me know when we've got to go.

WIFE: OK. [Kisses him on forehead.]

Had the wife simply asked if they could go out, she would've gotten a "too much to do, no time to do it" response, which is typical of Directors. She kept her proposal brief, considered his needs and wants, offered an alternatives, and "closed the sale" with a WIN/WIN result. If the wife had gone on and on about how *she* deserved a night out the result would have been quite different. If she just asks to go out without showing she knows her husband's needs, he is not going to go out as he sees no benefit. By following the patterns of persuasion she produced a WIN/WIN situation. This is a very easy presentation to make. Greater challenges exist, however, and for those we will unlock the door to powerful, effective presentations with the Seven Keys to a Successful Presentation.

The Seven Keys to a Successful Presentation

1. *Plan for a very brief presentation, but prepare for the potential need of a lengthy one*—Can you state your proposal in five minutes? Two minutes? Forty-five seconds?

Regardless of whether you are selling roses or Rolls Royces, you should be able to make your point in a *very* short amount of time. If you have never given this consideration, time your presentation to fit into each of the above time slots.

Brevity is a skill few salespeople possess. Because a large number of decision makers communicate in the Director style, it would be incredibly wise to learn to communicate your proposals in concise terms.

Paradoxically, because many people communicate in the style of the Amiable or Analytical, you must also be prepared to give a more detailed presentation. In addition, the Amiable will need to feel the warmth of an emotionally supportive presentation.

2. *State your objective briefly*—At the very beginning of your presentation, you need to state the exact reason for your meeting in terms of how you can be of value to your prospect.

• "John, the reason I'm here is to inform you of how you can save about $10,500 per year in secretarial costs by using our new software."

• "Janet, I've been tracking over 7,500 investments via computer for the last sixteen years and believe we can offer you a return of 17-23 percent per year based upon your goals and needs while preserving your capital."

• "Ted, I've thoroughly researched your present advertising campaign and have a proposal that, based upon computer-generated probabilities, will yield a profit of between 8 and 14 percent over what your gross receipts were in 1995."

By stating your exact objective in terms of the prospect's needs and benefits, you gain immediate interest and a focused frame of mind for the prospect.

Don't be afraid to let the prospect know what's in it for you. If you are a commissioned salesperson, tell the client. "John, I get paid on commission. This is important for you to know because it means that if you become dissatisfied with our service, we both lose. If you continue to make money using our investment program, we both win. So, will you promise to call me personally if there's anything I can do to help?"

Commissioned salespeople make their long-term money on renewing old clients' business or selling new products and services to previous clients. Therefore, commissioned salespeople *work harder* to have customer satisfaction than those on salary!

3. *Paint a vivid picture of the future resulting from acceptance of your proposal. Compare this to what the future will be like without the acceptance of your proposal*—What will it be like when they own your product? What will they see, hear, feel? What will happen if they fail to act? How will it hurt them? How is your proposal the solution to their problems?

Are we just telling them that they will see, hear, and feel good things for using our product or service, or are we making it a vivid, compelling experience? Compare these statements.

Software Sales

A. "Using our software will make your job much easier."

B. "Using our software will make your job so much easier, you'll feel like your computer is doing the work for you."

Car Sales

A. "You'll feel pretty darn good driving this car down the road."

B. "Can you imagine the girls looking to see who's driving this car down the road?"

Home Sales

A. "It'll make you feel good to know that this house is all yours."

B. "Can you imagine how you'll feel knowing you won't be throwing money out the window for rent? Every dollar you invest in your home will help *you*. You either gain ownership or get tax breaks. All people who become wealthy own their own homes. You're on your way."

Of course, you will need to create visions using your own product, service, or proposal. Get prospects to experience the *now* benefits they will have when they accept your proposal. You will not only want to paint a vivid picture for your counterpart, but create a movie for him to star in.

The movie also must illustrate the result of failing to act on your proposal. If a person feels no pain, he is unlikely to accept your proposal for goods or services. What will happen if he does *not* purchase your service?

This critical element of stirring the imagination can change a no into a yes. In the story *A Christmas Carol,* old Ebenezer Scrooge is taken into the future and shown what his life will be like *if* he does not change and listen to the spirit. It is this same concept that is so effective in the persuasion process.

When you show what the person will lose if he does not act on your proposal and then show the vivid picture of what he will get if he accepts your proposal, he almost always will accept your proposal. Scrooge would not have changed his ways if he was not shown his future. The person you are trying to persuade will not change his ways if you do not show him his future without your services, ideas, or products.

To put it simply, you discover the person's problems and pain. You then eliminate those problems and pain. You become a hero and the person will always be your friend!

4. *Be congruent*—Make certain your nonverbal communication matches your verbal presentation. When communicating about a positive, exciting experience, a smile is very appropriate. When communicating a sober or somber message, a smile creates incongruity, and a lack of belief on the part of the listener.

Your tone of voice, volume, pitch, and rate should be appropriate to the context of your presentation.

Many proposals are discounted due to incongruity on the part of the persuader. The Master Persuader refines his presentation so it is congruent with his nonverbal communication.

5. *Use presuppositions*—One of the most powerful presentation

tools you have is the presupposition. *Obviously*, you will have more success in the persuasion process if you use presuppositions. *Luckily*, you have an opportunity to practice using presuppositions before the persuasion process begins. *Obviously, luckily, fortunately, happily* are all words that presuppose something.

• "How interested are you in improving your persuasive abilities?" This question presupposes your interest. The question is not "are you interested in improving your persuasive abilities?" The question is "how interested are you?"

• "Are you *still* interested in making more money in the stock market?"

• "If we could find the perfect home for you, *how willing* would you be to spend a little more money?"

• "*When* did you *decide* to consider another company to be your office supplier?"

• "*When* would you *begin* your investment program?"

• "Have you made your contribution *yet?*"

• "*When* would you want your subscription to *start?*"

Use presuppositions whenever you can. They are *obviously* very powerful. *When* will you *begin* writing some presuppositions on paper to fit your proposals and presentations?

6. *Use tie downs*—A tie down is a verbal device designed to gain agreement. You can use tie downs as many as two or three

times in your presentation in order to get agreement. This is often necessary if you have a prospect who is very quiet and you do not know how he feels about your proposal.

You can also use the tie down to gain agreement verbally on key issues of your presentation, or right before you close your presentation and ask your prospect to accept your proposal.

Tie downs are very effective if used only two or three times in your proposal.

- "You do want this home, *don't you?*"

- "This is a profit-making idea, *isn't it?*"

- "You will save money with this software, *won't you?*"

- "You can afford it, *can't you?*"

- "Antilock brakes are important, *aren't they?*"

Even more effective is the tie down that is used in response to something the other person says.

PROSPECT: I really like your program.

MP: Thank you. What do you like the most?

PROSPECT: It sure is a beautiful home.

MP: Isn't it?

PROSPECT: Can I get it in red?

MP: Would you want it in red?

PROSPECT: Could I take it home today?

MP: Would you want to take it home today?

The use of tie downs on occasion will salvage lost proposals and clinch those on the brink. Overuse of tie downs will make the prospect feel manipulated.

7. *Use client-centered thinking*—Every part of your proposal is important to the client if, and only if, it shows *what's in it for him*. Point after point in your proposal should be benefit on top of benefit for the prospect. Your "client" can be a prospect, your spouse, your boss, or anyone you're trying to help.

Your proposal must tell your prospect what it will do for him.

Very few people buying a car care that it has a 2.2-liter engine, fuel injection, or a turbocharger. The car buyer wants to know *what it will do for him* as far as performance, speed, passing ability, and gas mileage.

A new computer buyer doesn't care that a computer has 40 megabytes of memory, an extended keyboard, and so on. The computer buyer wants to know how the equipment can benefit him. What abilities does it have that he will use?

An effective way of determining the value of your statements is to ask yourself the question prospects will ask: "So what?"

POOR PERSUADER: Our company has $10 billion in assets.

PROSPECT: So what?

MP: Your investment in life insurance is 100 percent safe because we have more assets than any other life-insurance company in the country. Your family *will* receive benefits upon your death. *Obviously* the same cannot be said for other companies. You've made *a wise decision* in selecting this company.

PROSPECT: Wow.

POOR PERSUADER: Our money-market fund will pay you an extra ½ percent on your money.

PROSPECT: So what?

MP: Using our money-market fund for your IRA will earn you thousands of dollars more for your retirement because we are able to pay an extra ½ percent interest on your money.

PROSPECT: Wow.

POOR PERSUADER: This computer has a 40-megabyte hard drive.

PROSPECT: So what?

MP: As a writer, you will appreciate owning this computer because it will store all your pages of text, even a 1,000-page book, because it has 40 megabytes of memory.

PROSPECT: Wow.

Client-centered thinking shows that the Master Persuader cares. Everything the Master Persuader says is for the other person's benefit. The result, of course, is success in the persuasion process.

Key Points Outline: Powerful Presentations Made Easy

I. Plan for a very brief presentation, but prepare for the potential need of a lengthy one

II. State your objective briefly

III. Paint a vivid picture of the future resulting from acceptance of your proposal; compare this to what the future will be like without the acceptance your proposal.

IV. Be congruent

V. Use presuppositions

VI. Use tie downs

VII. Use client-centered thinking

PARADIGM OF PERSUASION

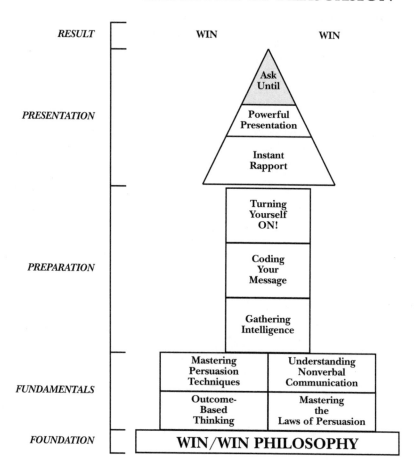

CHAPTER 11

Ask Until

We are interested in others when they are interested in us.
—Publius Syrus

The deepest principle in human nature is the craving to be appreciated.
—William James

'Tis a lesson you should heed,
Try, try again.
If at first you don't succeed,
Try, try again.
—W. E. Hickson

"Ask and you will receive," the wisdom of the Bible says.

In the persuasion process, especially in the subset of the sales process, we find that people often gain rapport, identify needs, clarify values, present their proposal, and then don't ask for commitment!

Research has shown that, on the average, in the buying process a person has to be asked five times before he says yes to a proposal. Unfortunately, 80 percent of all sales calls end with zero or one request for the prospect to commit. In relationships the same thing happens. We lay out all kinds of "hints" to be seen, then don't *ask!*

The entire purpose of the persuasion process is to get others to *take action*. Getting commitment and agreement from others is what this book is all about. It's what *you* want.

You only get paid in selling if you get that commitment. You only "get" a spouse after courting if you ask *until* the other says yes. If at any point the person who is asking quits, both parties lose (at least sometimes!).

Of course, between asking and asking *until* there are some challenges.

In the sales process:

"No."	"Can't afford it."
"Not interested."	"Don't need it."
"I'll think about it."	"I guess not."
"I only buy from my brother."	

In the relationship process:

"No."	"Too busy."
"I have a headache."	"Not interested."
"I have a boyfriend."	"Another time."

These are tough objections to overcome.

Resistance can be met and dealt with effectively *if* the rest of the persuasion process has gone well. If the Master Persuader has become the friend of his counterpart, if his counterpart needs the product or service, and if the Master Persuader has clearly outlined how accepting the proposal will greatly benefit the person, he will agree, unless a condition exists.

Conditions

A condition is anything that makes it impossible to persuade someone from his way of thinking.

• A beautiful woman (married) sits on a barstool in a hotel bar. A young man walks up to her and says, "Saw you sitting

here, and thought you might like to go out with me tonight."
She replies, "No thanks." In this case, the young man can persist all he wants, but he is fighting a condition. The woman is
married and will not do anything to harm the marriage.

• A young couple is standing in a beautiful home. They'd love
to be able to buy it. The real-estate agent asks them if they
want it. It's Open House day. "Yes, but we can't," they say. A
condition exists. The monthly payment is more than the couple's combined monthly income. It is absolutely impossible at
this time to proceed.

If a WIN/WIN result will come from your proposal and no
conditions exist, it is your responsibility as a Master Persuader
to ask the prospect to commit.

Condition is the heads side of the coin and *resistance* is tails.
Objection is another word commonly used by salespeople for
resistance.

Resistance

Resistance is as normal to the persuasion process as snow is
to Minnesota in January. There are six basic reasons why people will not buy your products or services.

1. They don't like you.
2. They don't trust you.
3. They don't need what you're proposing.
4. They don't have a sense of urgency.
5. They don't have the money now.
6. They don't have the authority to make the decision.

Dealing with Resistance

Resistance is often a red flag that flies when we don't build
rapport. In a relationship, resistance will occur when one
party is not convinced of the best of intentions by the other.

When affinity is in question, it is pointless to try to cope with the resistance. Before dealing with resistance you must be certain you have rapport, know the other person's needs and values, know that you have his best interests in mind, and finally know where you are guiding the communication process to.

If we have effectively accomplished that then we can attempt to deal with resistance. These are some excellent strategies for doing so.

1. *Get people to like you.*

The number-one reason why people don't buy from a salesperson is because they don't like the individual. This is a tough one to swallow but the opposite is also true. It is possible to build rapport and have the person still not like you. It is rare, however. Therefore, it is important to make sure you are *in rapport* when the request for agreement is made on your part. You can do this by using a nonverbal cue like crossing your legs or shifting your position in your chair and making sure the other person follows suit. This will let you know the person is in rapport with you *now,* which in essence is saying that he or she likes you!

Most people will buy from you *because* they like you. The law of friends comes into play here. The law of friends, you will recall, says, "When someone asks you to do something and you perceive that person to have your best interest in mind, and/or you would like him to have your best interests in mind, you are strongly motivated to fulfill the request."

As we develop rapport with others, identify needs, and discover values, they will like us. It is almost impossible to have rapport with someone and not have him like you! It's almost a contradiction in terms.

The simple fact of the matter is that, each year, Americans spend *billions* of dollars on products, services, and charities they've never heard of, will never use, and don't care about, but they do this because *they liked the person who asked them.*

2. *Get people to trust you.*

It may seem that this is the same as 1 above, but it is not. Can you think of people you like but don't trust? Of course! Can you think of people you don't like but trust? Yes, there are some of those people as well.

People are *more likely* to trust you if they do like you. However, aside from this, the best way to get people to trust you is to ensure that your nonverbal communication is consistent with your verbal communication.

The best way to gain credibility is to *be* sincere and *show it* through interest in others and their needs.

People who don't trust people they like tend to distrust their claims. The distrusted person exaggerates and overinflates statements. When making a claim it is important to back up that claim with facts and evidence.

3. *Make sure they need your product or services.*

If you are selling snowblowers in Phoenix, you are in trouble. However, if your product or service meets the needs of the other person, it is your job to show him that the benefits of owning your product *far outweigh* any negligible cost involved. When someone tells you, "I don't need X," what he really means is "you haven't explained what this will do for me in a way that makes me desire it more than the money I'd have to give you for it." Therefore, in your presentation, paint a vivid picture that excites people about what you can offer them.

The famous psychologist Abraham H. Maslow determined that all humans have the same general hierarchy of *needs.*

People also generally *want* certain things. Look at this list and see if you don't want most of them.

We all want:

more money	P	be respected
be liked	L	live longer
have fun	E	be happy
be praised	A	be smarter
be safe	S	be comfortable
be healthy	U	peace of mind
have control	R	be loved
self-esteem	E	more energy

We all want to avoid:

losing money	P	criticism
rejection	A	the unknown
failure	I	looking foolish
losing something	N	death

The method of enhancing the need for your product is showing how *painful* it will be for the prospect if he doesn't own your product and how much pleasure he will experience if he does own your product. This is done during the presentation. If you hear, "I don't need it," after your presentation, you probably lost the opportunity to produce a WIN/WIN result.

You can avoid the *pain* of hearing, "I don't need it," by planning your presentation effectively, and carefully evaluating values and needs *early* in the presentation process.

4. Get them to want it now!

What is the worst thing that could happen if the person doesn't buy your product or service?

• The old car could break down and cost thousands to repair.

• Interest rates could go up and the prospect could miss the greatest home-buying opportunity in years, spending thousands more later.

• His home could be robbed without a new security system.

• He could die before he's covered by a proper insurance policy.

If you do not stress the worst-case scenario in your presentation, you may not create a sense of urgency. During the presentation, you can also stress the best-case scenario. What does he get for taking action *now?*

5. *Make obtaining your product easy and affordable.*

Obviously, before walking in the door, you need to have multiple options available for financing. If the prospect wants your product, you should be able to work out a program for him and let him have it. Be very flexible.

For unskilled salespeople, asking for money is difficult. The reluctance to ask for money is one problem. The inability to respond to "I can't afford it" is an even more substantial challenge.

PROSPECT: I can't afford it.

MP: I understand. If you could afford it, would you want this car?

PROSPECT: Yeah, but I can't.

MP: You determined that you were able to deal comfortably with $260 per month. This car, which is what you obviously want, is $287 per month. Is there any way you could save 90 cents a day in another area to compensate for the difference?

If the prospect replies *no*, you have a condition. If he says *yes*, you have a sale.

Another exceptionally powerful method of dealing with price resistance is to use the point of resistance as a reason to buy. Here's an example:

PROSPECT: I really can't afford this car.

MP: The payments on this car would be $200 a month. For as many miles as you drive in a month, you're looking at $50 a month in gas. How much did you spend last year on repairs and maintenance?

PROSPECT: About $1,000.

MP: Your present car gets about half the gas mileage as this one. That means about $100 a month. So the question is, would you rather drive the brand new '97 model for $250 a month including gas, or your '79, which is getting more beat up every day, for $200 a month and maybe a lot more if you need major engine or transmission work?

The very point of resistance is normally an excellent reason to buy if it is properly reframed.

6. *Talk to the person with the authority to make a decision.*

This is the easiest of all to deal with. Simply make certain you have a decision maker before you make a presentation, *before* you leave the office in the morning!

Understanding the six reasons why people don't buy is valuable. Dealing with resistance is another challenge.

Additional Strategies for Dealing with Resistance

1. *Use the feel, felt, found formula.*

"John, I understand how you *feel*. Bill Johnson *felt* the same way. After he carefully evaluated the situation, and considered all possibilities, he went ahead with the proposal. Since then, he's *found* he has made nearly six thousand dollars in profits in four weeks using our program."

2. *Handle some objections in the presentation.*

If one specific objection is inherent to your product or service, bring it up and defeat it in your presentation.

3. *Ask what it would take to convince the prospect.*

"John, can I ask you a question? What would it take to convince you to move ahead with the proposal?"

4. *Use the old-fashioned way of dealing with resistance.*

    A. Ignore it the first time you hear it.
    B. Validate it. "I understand how you could feel that way. . . ."
    C. Make it final. "Is there any reason other than X that would preclude you from moving ahead with the proposal?"

D. Refocus the prospect's thinking. "If we could handle X, would you go ahead with it?"

Confirming

Ask until they say *yes.*

Zig Ziglar once said in a seminar that you will make a sale "when your *big* stack of benefits looks bigger to the prospect than his *tiny* stack of money." Zig was right. When it is overwhelmingly obvious to someone that completing a transaction with you will be to his great benefit, he will do business with you.

Confirming is called "closing the sale" by salespeople. However you may refer to it, the following are the most powerful methods of completing the persuasion process.

Six Powerful Ways to Close the Sale

1. *Assumptive Close*—The assumptive close is very powerful and can be used in almost every situation. The salesperson or persuader never asks specifically for approval. It is simply assumed.

MP: I'm glad you got a chance to get this house. What are your plans for the backyard?

MP: This car is definitely a wise choice. Will you be driving it most of the time, or will your wife?

MP: [With order blank in hand.] John, what is your correct address here? Will you want the machine delivered here or to some other location? Will the billing be sent here as well?

2. *Puppy-Dog Close*—A favorite way to confirm the sale is using the Puppy-Dog Close. Everyone knows that a surefire way to

sell a dog is to let someone take it home for two or three days. No one can bring the puppy back. He becomes part of the family. Of course, the Puppy-Dog Close is effective with other products as well. For example, copy machines are often sold with this technique.

MP: John, I'll have the new XJ-30 model delivered tomorrow. We will show your secretary how to use the machine for maximum efficiency. After ten days, I'll call you. If for any reason you decide it isn't everything we talked about, I'll take it back and absorb any cost. Is that fair enough?

3. *Alternative-Choice Close*—This is probably the best close the Master Persuader can select. Very simply, the prospect is asked to choose between two options in the confirming process.

MP: Will you be wanting the stick shift or the automatic?

MP: Will you be paying cash or financing?

MP: Would you want it in red or blue?

4. *Sharp-Angle Close*—The Sharp-Angle Close is a specialized close to be used when the prospect asks, "Can it do X?" "Can you get it in Y?" "Will it give me Z?" The answer to each question is the sharp angle: "If it does X, do you want it?" "If I can get it in Y, will you take it?" "If it gives you Z, will you try it?"

PROSPECT: We need the hardware installed, up and running, by December 1st. Can you do it?

MP: If we can guarantee operation by December 1st, will you approve the order today?

5. *Secondary-Question Close*—This close is a variation of the Alternative-Choice Close, but is certainly equally effective. It takes a focused train of thought to use this option.

MP: Obviously, the only decision to make here is how soon you will start enjoying the increased savings by using this software package. By the way, will you want two copies of the instruction manual, or one?

The formula for the Secondary Question Close is as follows:

A) State the major decision (which is the "primary question" in the prospect's mind) as a benefit to the prospect.
B) Continue speaking between the major decision and asking the secondary question.
C) State the secondary question as an alternate-choice question.

6. *Future-Pace Close*—A powerful close you can learn to use is the Future-Pace Close. You confirm the sale on the picturesque future you created for the prospect.

MP: With your help, we can literally save a large number of children's lives and indeed make their lives better. What kind of corporate sponsorship should we include you with?

Entire books have been written on the process of closing the sale. Some of the better ones that I would recommend are included in the bibliography.

To bring the persuasion process to a close, you must offer what you have to offer and ask for what you want in return. With all the work you have put into reaching your objectives, you should not allow yourself to fall short in the final moments of the persuasion process. *Ask until* you get *yes*.

Ask until does *not* mean to ask the same question redundantly. It entails responding to feedback, meeting the prospect's concerns, assuring the prospect of his benefits for the money, and asking again.

Exhaust all possible means for a WIN/WIN result. If at any time a WIN/WIN result cannot be met, then a condition exists that you may not be able to overcome.

For the most part, however, asking for confirmation of the proposal in and of itself will dramatically increase positive results in the persuasion process.

Key Points Outline: Ask Until

I. Conditions

II. Resistance

III. Dealing with resistance
     A. Get people to like you
     B. Get people to trust you
     C. Make sure they need your product or services
     D. Get them to want it *now*
     E. Make obtaining your product easy and affordable
     F. Talk to the person with the authority to make a decision

IV. Additional strategies for dealing with resistance
     A. Use the feel, felt, found formula
     B. Handle some objections in the presentation
     C. Ask what it would take to convince the prospect
     D. Use the old-fashioned way of dealing with resistance

V. Confirming

VI. Six powerful ways to close the sale
     A. Assumptive Close

B. Puppy-Dog Close
C. Alternative-Choice Close
D. Sharp-Angle Close
E. Secondary-Question Close
F. Future-Pace Close

PARADIGM OF PERSUASION

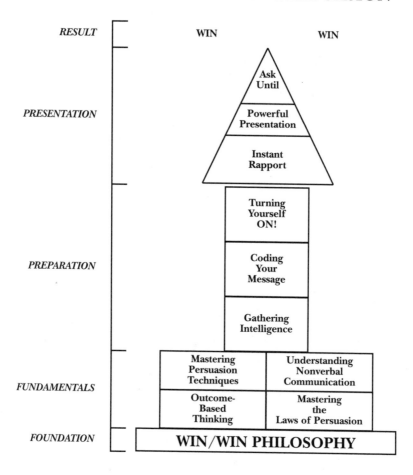

CHAPTER 12

WIN/WIN

Relationships. Life is about relationships, isn't it? Would it be more accurate to say that life is about developing harmonious relationships with others?

When I got married, my dear grandmother gave me a shocking piece of advice. She said, "Marriage is 90-10, not 50-50. You give 90 percent, and expect 10 percent." For some reason I didn't understand that at the time. I do now. Thankfully, I listened to her!

You can enforce 50-50 relationships. If you go to work, do exactly what is required of you, and get paid, you have a 50-50 relationship. There is nothing wrong with a 50-50 relationship. We need them! We need to be able to go to the service station, fill up with fifteen dollars' worth of gas, and pay the cashier fifteen dollars!

For relationships to transcend this level, we need to give more, without the expectation of a greater return. In other words, 90-10 needs to be given in faith. One of two things will happen.

First, it's very possible the other person will not see the benefits of your love and friendship (or service in a business sense) and will not reciprocate. Then you will have the opportunity to continue giving 90-10 or search for another relationship that will be more rewarding for you.

Second, it's just as possible the other person will see the love and friendship that you are bestowing upon him. He might then reciprocate out of the same unconditional love and friendship. This is then the beginning of something very special.

In business, if all we are concerned with is what we get out of a transaction, we will not gain the person's trust and repeat business. Using the techniques in this book, you can sell almost anything to almost anybody. This gets you a customer. The only way to *retain* that customer is to fulfill the promises you make.

Focusing on the other person's needs, values, and desires will allow you to act from the highest ethical levels. You will be determined to do what is in the other person's best interest.

WIN/WIN of course requires that you win as well. It is unwise to enter into transactions and relationships where you do not win. You cannot maintain self-esteem as a martyr. You cannot help people if you do not benefit from your relationships. You *must* feel satisfied about your relationships. The strategies you have learned in this book have given you the ability to make sure this happens.

WIN/WIN is more than an idealistic philosophy. WIN/WIN is an absolute necessity. If we do not create value for people they will not want to do business with us. If you do not fill the needs and wants of those with whom you are in relationships, both parties will lose. WIN/WIN is the *only* way to do business and the *only* way to maintain positive relationships.

WIN/WIN as you can see is a "life philosophy." It does not ensure that someone will love you. Nor does it ensure that you will get someone's business that you want. What it does do is give you the best opportunity.

The "no deal" is also a very important part of the WIN/WIN philosophy. If someone is not going to win, then there must be a "no deal." It's very possible that two people do not belong in a relationship with each other for any number of reasons. If this is true, then the only way that both parties can win is to have a "no deal." Always be willing to say no if someone is going to get hurt.

In Appendix A you will read about ethics and the problems of ethics in the persuasion process. Keeping the WIN/WIN philosophy as your bench mark will help you make ethical decisions.

This completes the first part of this book. If you would like to be even more influential in the communication process then read on and learn about *how* communication works and *how* what you communicate is perceived by others. You have a chance to take your communication to a new level. What is taught in part 2 of this book is understood by very few and practiced by even fewer.

You will learn how we are manipulated by the media, politics, and other aspects of life. You will learn about the programs that are making your brain "run." You will be able to quickly discover how other people have been "programmed" to give and receive information.

Before you go on to part 2, look at the chart, "Paradigm of Persuasion," and be certain you completely understand its various aspects. (This means that you understand it well enough to teach it to someone else!)

Now, you are ready for the next step. Get ready to move the universe!

PART II

Mastering Advanced Persuasion Techniques

CHAPTER 13

The Structure of Persuasion

Of all the creatures on Earth, only man was designed to
communicate effectively.   —Kevin Hogan

After mastering the material in the first part of this book, you
will be ready to begin learning the structure of persuasion.
The structure of persuasion is to the communicator what the
blueprints of a house are to the builder. You see an entirely
new picture. You see and hear different things in the communication process than other people do. It is at this point that
you begin to study for your "first-degree black belt in persuasion."

If you are uncertain about anything you have learned at this
point, return to that chapter and gain a complete understanding in that specific area. Part 2 of this book requires a
working understanding of the first twelve chapters! When you
understand the structure of persuasion, you will be able to
persuade almost anyone of almost anything as long as it does
not conflict with his most inner-core beliefs.

In order to influence others on this level, we first must
understand a useful and practical model of communication.

There are a number of communication models available to us. We will focus on a communication model based on the technology of Neuro-Linguistic Programming and hypnosis.

To begin, we will gain understanding of a few key components of the model before actually coming to the model itself. (Unlike the father on Christmas morning, we will read the instructions *before* we put the toy together!) First, we look at how physiology, internal representations, and states of mind interrelate.

1. *Physiology*—As you sit reading this book, you have a certain *physiology.* You are sitting in a certain way, breathing in a certain way, and some muscles may be tense, others relaxed. Physiology is *not* simply posture. It includes all physical action and inaction at each given moment. Physiology also includes our actual body position as well as the position of our legs, arms, hands, and fingers. Physiology finally includes the physical position and the movement of our eyes.

2. *Internal Representations*—At any given moment, your *internal representations* can be made up of the components of your five senses: visual, auditory, kinesthetic (feelings, touch), smells, and tastes. There is also a sixth representation called auditory digital. This is your internal dialogue. Specifically, *internal representations are configurations of information created and stored in the mind after being "run through" internal processing filters.* When you think of your "home" or "office," you are remembering an internal representation. When you imagine something you have not ever seen, you are constructing an internal representation.

3. *States*—Our state of mind is a combination of our internal representations and our physiology at any given moment. States can last for seconds or days.

$$physiology + internal\ representations = state$$

A person's state of mind, therefore, is the sum of all neurological processes in an individual at one moment in time. *The state one is in will filter or affect the final result of our interpretation and understanding of any experience we have at that moment.*

Example 1

You have just won the lottery. The phone call to the state office has confirmed it. You've won $1,000,000. STATE = JOY.

Your spouse walks in the door and tells you that the family car has a brand-new dent in it—$200 damage. How do you respond? If you're like most people, you'd respond, "Big deal! We just won $1,000,000!"

Example 2

You've had a very frustrating day at the office. Everyone was in a bad mood due to news of upcoming layoffs. You get home after a slow rush-hour traffic jam. STATE = FRUSTRATION and IRRITATION.

Your spouse walks in the door and tells you that the family car has a brand-new dent in it—$200 damage. How do you respond? If you're like most people, you'd respond, "Oh geez, now what else is going to go wrong today?"

Notice that the external event is *identical* in both situations. The behavior of the individual, however, is dramatically different. The reason the behavior is different is because the state of mind is different. Therefore:

$$state \longrightarrow behavior$$

In addition, the individual whose state of mind is JOY will accept and encode incoming stimuli in a different way than the same individual whose state of mind is FRUSTRATION. The internal representations of stimuli vary according to state because we filter and process information differently in various states. In the examples above, the information about the dented car can be encoded in dozens of ways. For example:

"When bad things happen, there is always something much better that comes along with them."

"Not only do I have to deal with idiots at work and on the highway, I have to deal with idiots in my home!"

Two very different interpretations are coming from an identical external stimulus. There are many more interpretations and conclusions that can come from the same situation. The interpretations are encoded with all the factual events and stored in memory with all the associations intact. When these events are recalled they tend to be "state dependent." The person will not only recall actual events but his interpretation of those events and, more impressively, the feelings he had at the time of the original events.

In the persuasion process our goal is to associate our idea, service, or product with the other person's favorite or target states. Whatever those states are that the person is constantly striving to attain need to be inextricably linked to whatever idea, service, or product you are proposing. This is how most advertising on television works and in fact is how the media is able literally to program our minds. With the realization that we want to associate our ideas with a person's target states in order to persuade, we can continue.

If you want someone to take you to a movie, you simply ask him what his favorite movie was. Ask him to tell you what was so incredible about it. As he tells you, note specific phrases he uses to describe his feelings.

". . . It was so intense when he saw the criminal. . . ."

Assuming this was the "peak experience" in the movie for this person, you can then use this information to suggest a similar experience in seeing a movie tonight: "Now, nothing is going to ever be as *intense* as when he saw the criminal, but even if this movie is *half* as good, isn't it worth going?!"

This is how we help others to associate their "target states" with our way of thinking, our products, or our services. After you associate the person's "target states" with your idea, he will have to fight his innermost desires *not* to do what you are asking. This is the essence of persuasion.

World War II was a time when young men were "programmed" by the media (remember there were no televisions, only radio and newspapers) to attach great honor, loyalty, and pride to "stopping Hitler" and "going over 'there' to destroy the Axis powers." The media messages came quickly and effectively. Pride became linked to serving your country. Serving your country was linked to killing Nazis. Killing Nazis was linked to being a hero. Being a hero was linked to great status when you got home, and so on.

(It is clear that stopping Hitler *was* a critical point in history and that the world would be a *very* different place today had we not. We are not debating the morality of any war but how states are created in people's minds to encourage enlistment and the desire to follow orders and act as part of a larger unit.)

The Japanese used the same exact techniques to create the air-fighter Kamikazes. These individuals knew that if they died fighting the evil Allied powers they would have their reward in eternity. This reward was far greater than anything they could ever possess here on Earth. It was this set of created beliefs that programmed Axis flyers to kill without fear. When someone has no fear of dying and has only positive associations with sacrifice, he will do *anything* for whatever cause he is fighting for. This is one reason why the Axis nations were so powerful in World War II. The states induced in their people culturally and especially in their soldiers would create an unstoppable mind set.

World War II was, in this author's opinion, a "justifiable

war." Vietnam may have been another story. Without debating the point, why was Vietnam perceived as so very differently from World War II, in the minds of the young people being called upon to serve?

Pictures.

There were pictures in our homes, every night on the news, of young men getting limbs blown off and dying. It was up close, personal, and the first look at war the masses had ever seen. It was truly a disgusting sight watching friends and family being killed or dismembered. Our internal representations were no longer imagined. They were vividly created for us. We did not see a hero or a loyal American patriot. We were seeing kids getting killed. War took on a new meaning for those who watched. It would change the paradigm of war for a nation forever. All the "links" were changed. We no longer linked war with heroism, bravery, and loyalty, except in a secondary way. War was now linked with death, destruction, dismemberment and disgust. Never again would the people of America be "pro-war." The pain associated with war would be too great. The associations were changing culturally.

War is used as a frame of reference to consider states because it is so powerful. The cultural change of states in the masses' minds was incredible with the advent of television. War would forever more be a kitchen-table experience and one that America would not enter into quickly. The dissenters would be out in greater force as technology increased. In third-world countries, where televisions are scarce, the story would be different. These countries are still in the 1940s. The people of media-deficient countries can still be programmed to link honor, loyalty, bravery, and heroism with stopping the enemy. Today the most violent countries continue to be those with very little *visual* coverage. Television gave us pictures. The visual component of internal representations is very powerful. With this vivid understanding now in place, we can see how this information is all filtered in the mind and is altered in the brain to create our beliefs.

Internal representations are different when we filter and process information in different states; therefore, we must learn about information filters. War can bring the sounds of glory and visions of the red, white, and blue flying overhead, until we see the reality on the kitchen table. These state changes alter the information we hear from other sources. We will now consider the most significant filters in the brain that help shape our behavior and our perceptions.

Processes

Fortunately, we are not consciously aware of 100 percent of the activity and stimuli around us. Thankfully, we can only see within a certain band of light and hear within a certain range of sound. Thankfully, we cannot feel every atom or molecule brushing against our skin. If we were able to experience all of that sensory input, we would overload. Imagine what it was like when people first saw American boys getting slaughtered in Vietnam. Regardless of the morality of the war, the internal representations changed across the country.

There are three processes that help us focus on what is apparently important in any given situation.

1. *Deletion*

This occurs when we consciously and/or subconsciously pay attention to certain aspects of our experience and not others. It means we leave out certain sensory information. As stated above, this can be good. Without deletion, our brains would "tilt" or overload. However, there are parts of our original experiences that would be useful if they weren't deleted.

For example, avid Bible readers might delete information that does not completely support their specific beliefs. In search of information that agrees with their point of view, they will often not even consciously see contradictory data. (This, of course, is one reason why there are so many sects in the Christian faith. In fact, this is why all religions fragment when they are based upon written documents.)

2. *Distortion*

This occurs when we misrepresent data to ourselves, or in some way "blow it out of proportion." Distortion, like deletion, can be beneficial or limiting.

A salesman might tell his sales manager he's had a lot of good interviews, which the manager might distort to mean that many sales were made when, in fact, there were none, just "good interviews."

Whenever you visualize an event that has not occurred in reality (such as when using *future vision*), you are distorting sensory data for motivational purposes and this is obviously beneficial.

3. *Generalization*

This occurs when we draw conclusions based on one, two, or more experiences. Like deletion and distortion, generalization is a process that can have positive or negative results.

Someone who has a wonderful marriage may generalize that marriage is wonderful for all. Conversely, someone who marries and has a bitter divorce may generalize that all marriages are bad and destined for divorce.

All communication is affected by deletion, distortion, and generalization.

Let us consider a situation where an employee asked for a raise . . . and didn't get it:

BOSS: So, as you can see, you've done a good job, and we really do appreciate it. I simply can't give you any dollars. I'm sorry. Had your sales been better, I might have been able to do something.

(Employee goes home and explains what happened to spouse.)

EMPLOYEE: So, he really is a good guy, said I've done a *super job,* but it'll be a little while, maybe two to three months, before I get a raise.

In the above scenario, the employee completely *deleted* the reason for his not getting the raise—his lack of sales. He also *distorted* the boss's comments from a "good job" to a "super job." The boss's statement that he appreciated the good job the employee had done was *generalized* to "he is a good guy."

The processes of deletion, distortion, and generalization are common to all people of all cultures. These processes occur within an individual's "filters." There are several categories of filters. They include Meta Programs, Values, Beliefs, Attitudes, Decisions, and Memories.

Meta Programs

Meta Programs are among the deepest filters of perception. These internal sorting patterns unconsciously let us decide what we pay attention to. Meta Programs are, generally speaking, content free. Like a computer program, which "runs the show" but does not actually store information, your state will determine what will go into the Meta Program creating your internal representations.

In order to use a computer program effectively, you must understand how to use it. *In order to communicate with and persuade people effectively, you must understand what Meta Programs they use.*

Because Meta Programs are deletion and distortion filters that adjust our generalizations, we can predict others' states *if* we know their Meta Programs. If we can predict a person's state, we can predict that individual's *actions*.

There are about twenty-five Meta Programs that have been identified as sorting patterns for individuals. We will examine the Meta Programs that *most* affect the persuasion process.

We have already discussed two Meta Programs and their relationship with each other in chapter 7. The first Meta Program we discussed was the *assertiveness sort*. This sorting pattern determines a person's tendency to be extroverted or introverted.

The second Meta Program we discussed was that of the *internal-state sort*. This sorting pattern determines whether a person tends to be a dissociated thinker or an associated feeler.

You will recall that the programs interrelate to give us the four communication styles: Director, Socializer, Amiable, and Analytical. (About 38 percent of people are Socializers, 37 percent Directors, 13 percent Amiables, and 12 percent Analyticals.)

All Meta Programs exist on a continuum and are not *either/or!* Some people are *very* extroverted where others are just a bit on the extroverted side. Some people are completely emotional, often on the brink of irrationality. Others delete their feelings and become like Mr. Spock from the original "Star Trek" series. These two Meta Programs are greatly involved in the persuasion process, as are those that follow.

Direction Sort

The direction sort is very important to the persuasion process. Everything we do is either to gain pleasure or avoid pain.

away ◄──► toward

If we can determine whether people move *toward* rewards and goals or *away* from punishment and fears, we can motivate people more effectively. People who operate out of fear of loss (away) will not be motivated effectively by painting pictures of an adventurous future.

> What do you want in life?
> What do you want in a career?
> What do you want in a relationship?

People will answer these questions with what they want or what they are avoiding. Additionally, people may also move toward something in some aspects of their lives, and be avoidant in other aspects. Everything must be taken in context.

If you ask someone, "What do you want in _____?" and he answers in such a way that is neither toward or away, you must be more specific: "What will having _____ mean to you?" For example:

MP: What do you want in a car?

PROSPECT: Good gas mileage.

MP: What will good gas mileage mean to you?

PROSPECT: I'll save money.

MP: Would you like to look at gas-saving cars that will also keep your monthly installment down?

Frame of Reference Sort

The frame of reference sort reveals how people judge the results of their actions. Some people know they have done something well, for example, if someone tells them so. This is an *external* frame of reference. Other people just know (from a feeling or something they see or hear) inside that they've done something well. This is called an *internal* frame of reference.

internal ◄────► external and/or data

The third option in this sort is that of *data.* Many people will base their decisions and judge their actions on data. Data is not an internal feeling nor is it referring to other people. People who tell you actions or decisions are based on "data" or "guidelines" should be dealt with differently than those who use other people for their authority.

MP: How do you decide which car is best for you?

PROSPECT: Well, we used *Consumer Reports* to narrow it down and now we'll pick out the one we want.
(DATA SORT with INTERNAL check)

MP: How do you know whether to accept a proposal or not?

PROSPECT: I'll know. Now, what do you have to tell me?
(INTERNAL SORT)

MP: How do you know what organizations to donate to?

PROSPECT: I just ask my wife. That's her department.
(EXTERNAL SORT)

When people are new at something, they tend to have an

external frame of reference. As time goes by, they tend to move to an internal frame of reference. The more confident a person believes himself to be in a given context, the more the person moves toward an internal sort.

As a Master Persuader, you can use a person's frame of reference as support for accepting your proposal. You will know whether to appeal to the person's intelligence, testimonials, or objective data about your proposal.

Match/Mismatch Sort

Understanding the match/mismatch sort is critical to success in the persuasion process. When trying to understand or judge something, some people look for similarities. Others look for differences.

sameness ←——→ difference

- "What is the relationship between what you're doing this year in your career and what you did last year in your career?"

- "What is the relationship between the quality of employees you can hire this year compared to last year?"

- "What is the relationship among the boxes?"

Individuals who compare things are on the sameness end of the continuum. People who contrast things are on the difference end. The continuum is basically divided into four segments.

1. *Polarity*—Some individuals polarize just about everything that is communicated to them.

QUESTION: Nice day, huh?

POLARITY: I don't think so.

The polarity sorter automatically responds with the opposite of a communicated idea. If you wanted a polarity-sorter spouse to go to the store and do the shopping for you:

MP: Honey, you don't want to go to the store and do the shopping, do you?

POLARITY: I *do* want to go. You stay home.

2. *Mismatch/Exception*—The mismatch/exception responds to a statement in this fashion: "Well, *I don't think so . . . but* your idea does have some merit. Who knows, it may work."

3. *Match/Exception*—The match/exception responds to a statement in this fashion: "*Yes,* you're right, it does look like a good proposal, *but* it may not meet our needs."

4. *Match*—The matcher might respond like this: "Sure, I've seen proposals like this before. They're all alike. We won't be buying."

In order to meet your objectives, you must effectively fit your proposal into the match/mismatch sort.

Percentage of Americans in Each Sort

Polarity Sort	5 percent
Mismatch/Exception	25 percent
Balanced	10 percent

| Match/Exception | 50 percent |
| Match | 10 percent |

Another way to confirm your estimation of an individual's sort in this area is to determine how many jobs he's had in the last ten years. If he's had one or two, he falls into the match or match/exception part of the continuum. If he's had three or four, he falls into the balanced portion. If he's had five or more jobs in the past ten years, he probably falls closer to the polarity end of the continuum.

People who deal with polarity responders often are greatly annoyed and understandably so. The benefit is that the person is easily motivated. Simply mention to the person that you doubt he can do something. He will then do everything in his power to do whatever it is you said you doubted!

General/Specific Sort

The general/specific sort is also critical in understanding the persuasion process.

General sorters want an overview, the *big picture,* the "in a nutshell" communication. Specific sorters want details—lots of details.

General sorters are people who put things together before they read the directions. The general sorter gets annoyed when you go into great detail. He doesn't want to hear about the "irrelevant" points in a plan. Give him the big picture and you will win a friend. He tries to program the VCR or other electronic equipment without even looking at the manual.

Specific sorters read all the fine print. They want details. Specific sorters are great accountants. If you tell them the big picture and expect them to act on the big picture alone, they will feel that you are hiding something from them.

general ◄────► specific

If you are presenting a proposal to a specific sorter and you are able to match his sort, you will be in very good shape indeed. The specific sorter will appreciate the detail. The general sorter will go crazy if you bog him down with the details. As a rule, Directors tend to be general sorters and Analyticals tend to be specific sorters. Amiables and Socializers tend to be more balanced.

Convincer Sort

The convincer sort is valuable to those in both business and personal relationships. The convincer sort deals with what convinces you of something, then how long it takes to convince you of this.

1. How do you know when someone has done a good job? Do you have to:
  a. see or watch him do it?
  b. hear about how good he is at it?
  c. do it with him?
  d. refer to data in reference to him?

2. How often does someone have to demonstrate he can do something before you're convinced he can do it?
  a. Once.
  b. Two or more times.
  c. Often, over a long period of time.
  d. Continuously.

once ◄────► continuously

Knowing a person's convincer sort will make the management process much easier. Is your boss constantly checking up on you or is it his internal programming that compels him to make sure you are doing a good job over and over again? This is also valuable within the context of relationships.

Necessity/Possibility Sort

A necessity sorter does things because they are absolutely necessary. He feels he has to do them. The possibility sorter does things because he feels that he wants to. Do people do things because they feel they have to or want to?

necessity ⟷ possibility

Knowing whether people do things because they have to or because they want to can be a valuable persuasion tool. The type of question you might ask would be:

"Why did you go to work at the company you're currently at?"
"Why did you buy the house you currently own?"

If a person does something because he feels he has to, you can't talk to him about all the possibilities of trying something else. A person who does things out of the possibility of something wonderful happening is not likely to be motivated by hearing he "needs something."

Action Sort

How quickly can a person analyze a situation? How careful is he? An individual's opinion of himself can be drawn from this question: "When you come into a situation, do you usually act quickly after analyzing it, or do you do an in-depth study of all the consequences, and then take action?"

reflective ⟷ active

Affiliation Sort

Does a person prefer to work alone or with others? This can be a helpful piece of information, especially when persuading employees: "Would you prefer to work by yourself or with others for you to be the happiest?"

self ⟷ others

Exercise

Present your proposal to accommodate the individual's Meta Programs. These sorts are among the most important for the persuasion process. The entire purpose of using another person's Meta Programs in communication is to make your communication more acceptable and pleasing to the listener. The following exercise will help you familiarize yourself with them in greater detail.

Ask your spouse or a friend to let you determine his Meta Programs. After accomplishing this, propose something to him using his Meta Programs. Then propose the same thing to him using the *opposite* of his Meta Programs. Ask him how he responded internally in both cases. Have him write these thoughts down as you give your proposal.

After you have completed this exercise, review the Meta Programs used for persuasion below and be certain you understand each one before continuing.

Meta Programs for Persuasion

• Direction Sort—away ⟷ toward

• Frame of Reference Sort—internal ⟷ external and/or data

- Match/Mismatch Sort—sameness ◄───► difference

- General/Specific Sort—general ◄───► specific

- Convincer Sort—once ◄───► continuously

- Necessity/Possibility Sort—necessity ◄───► possibility

- Action Sort—reflective ◄───► active

- Affiliation Sort—self ◄───► others

Values

Understanding how Meta Programs are filters in the persuasion process, we are now ready to look at our next set of filters, called values.

Values, as we have previously discussed, are a key component in the persuasion process. Values are the next most important unconscious sorter after Meta Programs. Values allow us to conclude that what we are doing is right or wrong, wise or foolish, good or bad.

Remember the strategy to discover values:

1. "What is most important to you in X?"
2. "What else is important to you in X?"
3. "What else?"

Remember the method to design a hierarchy of values:

1. "Of A, B, C, D, E, and F, which is most important?"
2. "Which is the next most important?"
3. "Which next?"

Remember also the evidence procedure to find out how someone knows when he "has" a value:

"What specifically has to happen for you to feel (or have) X?"

Finally, remember the difference between ends values and means values. Ends values are internal states that an individual wants to move toward or away from (love, happiness, security, freedom, boredom, frustration). Means values are things that an individual wants that will help him toward or away from his ends values (money, cars, houses, travel, career).

Beliefs

The next filters we have are beliefs. We all have beliefs. Our beliefs are either self-chosen or they were indoctrinated into us. According to Tad James and Wyatt Woodsmall, authors of *Time Line Therapy*, beliefs are presuppositions that either create or deny our actions. Our beliefs actually control our behavior. They allow us to do certain things and deny our doing others. Each belief is hooked to a value. Each belief is a statement about how we see the world.

Beliefs are generalizations that are very important to us. We don't like people attacking our beliefs and we believe others should believe what we do or they are probably wrong. You wouldn't believe something if you didn't think it was right. A belief is not something concrete. Like values, they are inside each of us. Almost all beliefs are based on *emotion* and are virtually impenetrable by logical thinking.

The war against Iraq in January 1991 was started because one man, Saddam Hussein, believed that Kuwait should be annexed as part of Iraq. That one belief and the action taken on it caused the destruction of at least 150,000 Iraqi lives and about 100 U.S. and Allied lives. Many people tried to stop the destruction of life and property in Iraq, but Hussein believed that he had a right to do what he did—invade his neighbor, Kuwait. The more negotiators told him he was wrong, the more he defended his position. Beliefs don't change easily in most people. Although using persuasion technology can change the beliefs of others, it is, in this author's opinion, unethical to do so in almost all instances.

In the persuasion process, you will work *within* an individual's structure of belief. Most people are consciously aware of most of their beliefs.

Everything in communication is processed through beliefs. When your beliefs interfere with the persuasion process, you will be unable to persuade the other person. You must meet a person at *his beliefs,* not yours. You can only influence a person if what you are saying is in synch with his beliefs.

Attitudes

The next filters are attitudes. Attitudes are a collection of values and beliefs around a certain subject. Most people try to change other people's attitudes without success. Attitudes cannot be changed without changing values first. Beliefs, as we mentioned, hang on values. Likewise, attitudes hang on beliefs.

Attitudes need to be dealt with in the persuasion process. Because attitudes occur in the conscious mind, the instinct is to deal with them consciously. Unfortunately, we normally have little success in changing attitudes alone. Telling someone to change his attitude never works—never. Let's consider a specific value and how beliefs create an attitude.

Example

Racial prejudice is an attitude. In order to persuade someone to accept people of other ethnic groups, you need to do more than tell him that people are all the same.

Value: Security
Belief A: When I'm around people I know, I'm secure.
Belief B: All the people I know are the same color as me.
Belief C: When I see people of another color, they scare me.

Belief D: People of other colors don't like me because of my color.

Belief E: I don't want to get hurt by people, so I stay away from people of different colors.

Attitude: People of other colors might be OK, but they make me nervous.

The beliefs are hung on a value. The above beliefs are *distorted*. Beliefs come from:

1. *Environment,* including peer group and parents.
2. *Events,* including media.
3. *Knowledge.*
4. *Past results.*
5. *Self-created,* including acts of faith.

In the above example, the value of security is certainly reasonable, but the beliefs that hang on the value have been distorted in at least one of the five areas noted. You cannot change this belief in another person with logical thinking. It is irrational. Beliefs have nothing to do with reality. They are beliefs because they are *not* facts or concrete. You can see how important beliefs will be in the communication process.

Decisions and Memories

Decisions and memories are the fifth and sixth filters for communication. Some decisions and memories lie deep in the subconscious. Others are easily accessible in the conscious mind.

Decisions affect the persuasion process in an interesting way. Past decisions are full of content (unlike Meta Programs, which are content free). A person's past decisions will come into play in a couple of different ways.

1. *Success/Failure*—When an individual makes a decision within a specific context, that individual will experience certain degrees of success or failure. The most important of these successes or failures will impact future decisions. For example, if a man finally decides to ask a woman to marry him, only to be rejected, he will remember that decision as a failure and be hesitant to ask someone else.

2. *Consistency*—We tend to make decisions consistent with the decisions we've made in the past. You will recall the law of consistency from chapter 3. Because we have an internal desire to be consistent, and indeed can't do anything inconsistent with our core values, we will decide on issues in the future based on this information.

Memories, like decisions, are 100 percent content full. (Meta Programs on the other hand are virtually content free.) Memories, of course, play a critical part in the persuasion process. Everything we do is filtered through our memories. If we've had good experiences with salespeople in the past, we will likely enjoy meeting with them. If we've had good experiences with relationships, we will want more of the same. The converse is also true.

Because all these filters distort, delete, and generalize, the same can be said for memories. Whether someone remembers events accurately or not becomes irrelevant. It is *how* he remembers events compared to the context of present communication that affects his internal representations, and thus his states and behaviors.

Please study the Structure of Persuasion Model here. This model is based on the NLP model of communication as noted earlier.

Structure of Persuasion Model

Sender (A) transmits message to receiver (B)

Message runs through filters that *delete, distort, generalize:*

1. Meta Programs	2. Values	3. Beliefs
4. Attitudes	5. Decisions	6. Memories

Filtered message meets B's (present) *state of mind*

A ———▶ / ———▶ B

State of mind alters, eliciting a new behavior

A —▶ / —▶ B —▶ new state —▶ new behavior

Note: state = physiology + internal representations

At the top of the model there is a stimulus. This can be any event or communication. It can be directed at the individual hearing the message, or it can be indirect. The event is then distorted, and experiences some deletion and generalization after it passes through the Meta Programs, Values, Beliefs, Attitudes, Decisions, and Memories of the listener.

The filtered message integrates with the individual's present state of mind (which, as you know, is the sum of an individual's physiology and internal representations). A new state of mind is generated, which, of course, will elicit a new behavior.

The most effective way to persuade someone is to use the same "programming" that he processes information with. When one computer communicates with another via a communications device, it is difficult for them to transmit and receive messages if they don't run on the same system (programming or software). Similarly, we will need to match our counterparts' values, beliefs, attitudes, and especially their Meta Programs if we are to be completely effective in the persuasion process.

We must make our proposal to others using their "system" made up of Meta Programs, Values, Beliefs, Attitudes, Decisions, and Memories, as we know it, to have optimum success. The only way we can determine this information is through the use of questions. Questions will help us immensely in determining values. In the next chapter, we will gain more experience in the area of questions.

Key Points Outline: The Structure of Persuasion

I. States
        A. physiology + internal representations = state
        B. state ⟶ behavior

II. Processes
        A. Deletion
        B. Distortion
        C. Generalization

III. Filters
        A. Meta Programs
        B. Values
        C. Beliefs
        D. Attitudes
        E. Decisions and Memories

IV. Structure of Persuasion Model

CHAPTER 14

Master Persuader Part I

WIN/WIN or NO DEAL. —Stephen R. Covey
The Seven Habits of Highly Effective People

The Master Persuader only considers one outcome: WIN/WIN or he doesn't make a deal. The Master Persuader has an objective. He reaches it. The Master Persuader has a wide range of responses to any situation. He has thought them through well in advance in most cases. The Master Persuader is a master of monitoring feedback and has the flexibility needed to respond accurately and effectively.

Others view the Master Persuader as charismatic and concerned. They are amazed at how he can always find a plan to reach a goal. He exudes confidence.

The Master Persuader was *not* born that way. The Master Persuader started out clumsily just like everyone else. One thing was different, though. He gained the ability to *monitor* and *respond appropriately*. This a skill, and skills can be learned. The preceding chapter contained the information you need to learn what makes any individual "tick." You can now find a person's "hot buttons" with the greatest of ease. Just understanding filters alone will not allow us to persuade someone to our way of thinking, however. This chapter will add the necessary flexibility and precision to the equation. It will take time to attain command over these skills. Be patient.

The ability to be flexible is one of the most critical to the persuasion process. When you have an objective in communication and you see that you are not reaching that objective, it is crucial that you change your approach as quickly as possible.

Determining Meta Programs

One of our objectives as Master Persuaders is to gather as much data as possible about our communicating partner in the shortest amount of time possible.

We do *not* have an opportunity to give everyone we meet a personality test. We don't have time to find out a hierarchy of values in all of our acquaintances. We don't have an opportunity to learn all the Meta Programs of each individual we need to help. Therefore, we need to be skilled at asking questions that give us as much valuable data as possible.

Let's return to an example used in chapter 9 and this time determine what Meta Programs each person is using to process information.

A recently married husband and wife are trying to decide on where to go on vacation.

HUSBAND: *What do you want in a vacation?*

WIFE: Hm. To get away from all the hustle and bustle. To get out from under all the housework and just relax.

HUSBAND: *What's the perfect place to go for a vacation?*

WIFE: Oh, I don't know. I've never given it that much thought.

I used to just go with a few friends and go camping.

HUSBAND: *What exactly did you like about camping?*

WIFE: Well, I guess I liked being out in the fresh air, sitting by a campfire, and just talking. *What about you, honey? What did you have in mind?*

HUSBAND: Well, I wanted to go to Las Vegas for a week and play some cards, see some shows, and have a good time.

WIFE: Hm. I've never been to Vegas. I don't know that I'd like it much. Seems like you're leaving the rat race to get to a bigger rat race.

HUSBAND: I know exactly how you feel. I used to think that way until I went and was surprised at how fun it really is.

WIFE: I guess I'd really like to avoid all the problems of city life on a vacation.

HUSBAND: Well, maybe we can compromise. *Would you be willing to do that?*

WIFE: Well, sure, I suppose.

HUSBAND: What if we went somewhere where the air is fresh and clean, the pine trees smell beautiful, there aren't a lot of people, and I can still have fun, too. *How would that be?*

WIFE: Well, sounds good to me. Where would we go?

HUSBAND: Lake Tahoe.

WIFE: I've never been there. I don't know if I'd like it.

HUSBAND: Remember when you used to go camping with

your friends and sit around the campfire and smell the fresh air?

WIFE: Yeah.

HUSBAND: Can you imagine doing that with thousands of beautiful pine trees and snowcapped mountains in the background?

WIFE: Yeah.

HUSBAND: That's Lake Tahoe. Honey, let's go to Tahoe, get away from it all, and relax.

WIFE: OK. Let's go.

Meta Programs come into play in the above example as you can see. Go back through all the Meta Programs in the previous chapter. It's important that you *do* this. The husband and wife had different *direction sorts*. Who was moving away? Away from what? How do you evaluate the wife on the *affiliation sort* and the *action sort?* What would you guess is her communication style? Why?

Exercise 1

In implementing your ability to discover values, needs, beliefs, and Meta Programs into your daily life, begin slowly. Focus on identifying one Meta Program per day. Each day, listen to all communications and learn what Meta Programs people are using to sort with. Within two to three weeks, you will find yourself subconsciously doing this and responding appropriately.

Exercise 2

Tune in every night to a "M*A*S*H," "Cheers," or "Star Trek" rerun. Select another program if you like. Make a copy of the Meta Programs for Persuasion list and then use it to analyze each of the main characters in the show and learn how they sort. Additionally, determine the communication style for each character. This will be fun and will help teach your subconscious mind to recognize Meta Programs much more quickly.

Precise Questions

How/what questions are superior to all other kinds of questions when you are attempting to gain helpful information in the persuasion process. They produce the information you need to discover values and needs. You can see the laserlike results you will obtain when you use questions modeled on the following. Although many of these examples are set in a "sales-prospect" relationship, they work just as effectively in love and friendship relationships as well.

Value Discovery

"What do you want in a _____?"
"What's important to you about _____?"
"What do you value about _____?"
"What will having _____ do for you?"

Decision Discovery
(how people actually decide to accept your proposal)

"How did you decide you wanted _____?"
"When you bought your last _____, what were the deciding factors involved?"

Resistance Discovery

PROSPECT: I'm not interested.

MP: Is there any *reason* in particular?

PROSPECT: I'm not interested.

MP: What, specifically, could cause you to change your mind?

PROSPECT: I'm not interested.

MP: What, specifically, would I need to do to convince you to be interested?

PROSPECT: Call me back in six weeks.

MP: How will things change in six weeks?

PROSPECT: Call me back in six weeks.

MP: What, specifically, will be different in six weeks?

Combining these types of questions with questions to determine Meta Programs (discussed in the last chapter) will produce powerful results.

Working Within the Prospect's Programming

Once Meta Programs have been elicited, we can utilize the other person's programming by working within it. In order to understand this clearly, we will examine common Meta Programs and questions that can be used to close the persuasion process successfully. Here is a more advanced version of the vacation persuasion above.

HUSBAND: [Has determined that wife sorts by "moving away" from things.] . . . and knowing that you don't want to be around all of these problems and that you want to get away from the rat race on your vacation, where don't you want to be specifically?

WIFE: I don't want to be in a big city. I don't want to be where I'm going to be bothered. I don't want a lot of stress.

The husband then leads the wife to his solution, as he did above. He offers Lake Tahoe as a solution, and the wife agrees.

For another example, imagine that the person you are transacting with sorts by external data (the *Consumer Reports* reader as an example). You would proceed in a manner similar to this:

MP: What constantly amazes me is people who will act on gut instinct or check with a friend about what kind of car to buy. People will spend thousands of dollars without having any objective criteria to base their decision on. Isn't that ridiculous?

PROSPECT: Utterly.

MP: That's why I'm excited to show you this month's issue of *Consumer Reports,* where it rates our model as the best model in the price range. Now *that* is exciting, isn't it, to *know* that you are getting the best, instead of having someone tell you that?

Let's consider what to do if your prospect is a mismatcher. She tends to disagree with everything you say.

MP: It probably won't make any sense for you to make a decision to buy today, will it?

PROSPECT: Well, I wouldn't go that far. Today is just fine.

What if your prospect is a general sorter of information? You certainly won't be giving details to this person if you want him to accept your proposal.

MP: . . . and of course, the details will work themselves out. What you see here is that this resolution will meet the key criteria the company has set up. We'll let the people involved in the project clean up the details.

Imagine that you are dealing with a person who needs to see something several times before she is convinced it will work regularly.

MP: Now, just think what it's going to be like after you see this widget saving you 4 to 7 percent on your operating costs day in and day out, hour after hour, minute after minute.

PROSPECT: How do you know?

MP: Well, I could tell you that twenty other businesses have saved 4 to 7 percent, but I won't. I will tell you that Johnson Manufacturing used this product for ninety days before they were convinced that it would save them at least 4 percent. That hasn't stopped them from keeping up on its efficiency, however, as they make certain they are getting these consistent results every day. And then there is Wilson Equipment. They are saving about 6 percent off of their costs. It took quite a while for them to be convinced that the widgets actually worked. Today they couldn't be happier. In fact, you can call Rachel Wilson over there and check with her. Then there is . . .

Assume you have a conversation with someone who is only interested in doing what is necessary or those things he *must* do instead of what he could do.

MP: . . . and of course it really is necessary to carry one-quarter-million dollars of life insurance in this day. Isn't it amazing how people will hope that things will work out when in reality they don't even take care of their basic needs?! What is wrong with people?

What we are attempting to accomplish by operating within a person's programming system is to present our point of view in a fashion that is precoded for acceptance on the part of the other person. Using this kind of flexibility in our presentations will bring us strong, successful results. If we neglect people's Meta Programs, we are communicating underefficiently. By utilizing our understanding of Meta Programs, we can guide people, with questions, toward almost any objective or proposal.

Remember, when you possess the power to open people's minds and persuade them to your way of thinking, you accept the responsibility of producing a WIN/WIN result or no deal. Anything short of this result is foolish to enter into. When you consider just what a Master Persuader is, the following all come to mind.

Qualities of a Master Persuader

I. Uses Outcome-Based Thinking
    A. Sets goals for his communication
    B. Uses sensory awareness to determine if he's moving toward his goal

C. Has the flexibility to change any approach that doesn't work

II. Accepts responsibility for his communication
  A. If the Master Persuader's counterpart shows resistance, is responsible for changing the directionof the process
  B. Understands that the response he gets from the other person is the primary concern

III. Since mind and body are part of the same system and directly affect each other, is aware of both verbal and non-verbal communication at all times

IV. Responds flexibly in all communication; doesn't necessarily communicate in his own style—communicates in the style of those he encounters

V. Is mentally capable of Precision Thinking.
  A. Hears, "Things are great, terrible, wonderful, horrible, good, bad, too much, too expensive, too many," etc., and mentally responds, "Compared to what?"
  B. Hears, "They say, people say, the Church says, the White House says," etc., and mentally responds, "Who specifically?"
  C. Hears, "I can't, shouldn't, mustn't," etc., and mentally responds, "What would happen if you could?" or "What stops you?"
  D. Hears, "Always, never, all, none, every," etc., and mentally responds, *"Always? Never? All? None? Every?"*

VI. Doesn't act as though he knows it all; can appear to be ignorant of certain knowledge when it is advantageous in the persuasion process

VII. Avoids becoming competitive with those with whom he communicates

VIII. Learns something from everyone, be it the process of communication or the content of the communication; therefore, is always truly interested in people

IX. Never gets taken advantage of nor takes advantage of others: WIN/WIN or no deal

CHAPTER 15

Master Persuader Part II

In part 1 of this book, we covered the basics of proxemics and nonverbal communication. Now, we will look at additional distinctions, techniques, and strategies that will make a powerful impact in the persuasion process. This short but important chapter will help you fine tune your already impressive knowledge of persuasion.

Vocal Cues

In the sales process with only one or two people involved aside from yourself, modeling other people's speaking rate and volume are excellent ways to gain rapport. However, in a formal setting such as a meeting room or any other setting for public speaking, we are unable model each person in the room. Therefore we need to consider the most effective ways to build credibility and respect for the speaker. The following three generalities can be made for most public speakers and their vocal characteristics.

1. *Women* need to lower their pitch about one octave to be perceived as more professional. Moderate speech rate is prop-

er for most settings. High-pitched voices tend to be perceived as weak and annoying. By lowering the pitch the woman gains respect. Barbara Walters, Diane Sawyer, Cokie Roberts, Sue Herrara, and Oprah Winfrey all use midrange pitch and are all respected journalists and television personalities. Can you think of any successful women in similar roles who use high-pitched voices? There are very few.

2. *Men* need to lower their pitch about one-half octave to be perceived as more powerful. Think of men who have pleasant personalities but high voices. Men who speak with a higher pitch are seldom respected and often perceived as "too feminine." Ted Koppel, Dan Rather, Morley Safer, Peter Jennings, Tom Brokaw, and Hugh Downs are among men who use mid- and lower-range pitch very effectively. In doing so, they have enhanced their credibility and communication style.

3. *Both sexes* need to speak in longer sentences. Short, choppy sentences may make good print copy, but they don't add to the quality of a public presentation. The only man who has mastered the short and choppy sentence is Paul Harvey. Many imitators have come along, but they never last. Instead of trying to emulate a style that has only one effective communicator, model the many that are effective. Watch the news at night and determine the length of sentences your favorite commentators use compared to those that you do not like.

Understanding Eye Movement

A great deal of research has gone into the theory of eye movement and its interrelationship with internal representations. Apparently, the research has resulted in some consistent results that we will consider. The original research into eye movement was begun in the early 1950s by Dr. Ernest Hildegard. As a hypnotist he was very curious as to how the movements of an individual's eyes related to his behavior. In the 1970s the team of John Grinder and Richard Bandler did further research into eye movement.

The results of eye-movement studies have shown that people have a tendency to momentarily move their eyes to specific positions when remembering events, answering questions, when talking to themselves internally, experiencing feelings, and visualizing future events.

The following chart is divided into six areas. The chart allows you to determine what representational system a person is accessing according to the movement of his eyes.

The chart is viewed from *your* point of view, as you look at someone (who is right-handed).

Eye Accessing Cues

Vc–Visually constructed images–something never seen before	Vr–Visually remembered images–something he has seen before
Eyes: Up and to *his* right	Eyes: Up and to *his* left

(Defocused or staring eyes indicate visually recalled images [V].)

Ac—"Auditorily" constructed sounds or words— something never heard before	Ar—"Auditorily" recalled sounds or words from past sounds or conversations
Eyes: Level to *his* right	Eyes: Level to *his* left

K—Kinesthetic feelings (also smell and taste) sensing inner, past feelings or imagining future ones	Ad—Auditory digital— indicates talking to self, internal dialogue

Eyes: Down and to *his* right

Eyes: Down and to *his* left

(as you look at someone accessing)

A powerful way to enhance the communication process is to use the information on the Eye Accessing Cues chart in all your communications. For example, let's say you sell new cars.

MP: What exactly do you want in a new car, John?

PROSPECT: Well [eyes up and to his left], I want the nice red convertible you guys just came out with. [Eyes go down and to his right, then down and to his left.] But I want to get the best price possible. You know what I mean?

John has seen some kind of picture of the car he wants to buy (visual recall: Vr) and then he got some kind of feeling (kinesthetic: K) about the car. Finally, he had some internal dialogue (auditory digital: Ad) that prompted his concern about the price. So, in order to meet this prospect's needs, we need to *show* him the car, make him *feel* good about it, and answer his internal dialogue.

$$Vr + K + Ad \longrightarrow sale$$

MP: John, let's walk over here to the convertible you've got *pictured* in your mind. I know you'll *feel* great test-driving it. You'll be *asking yourself*, "Geez, why didn't I get this sooner?" after we're back.

When you can present your proposal to the prospect in his accessing sequence, you will nearly always end up with a WIN/WIN.

The most effective time to use this is in determining the decision-making sequence.

MP: John, about your home you currently own. What was the first thing that made you decide to buy it? Was it something you saw, or heard, or felt about it?

PROSPECT: [Eyes up and to his left.] When we saw it [eyes down and to his right], we fell in love with it. It looked so nice sitting on the property [visual recalled externally and kinesthetic].

MP: What was the very next thing that impacted your decision-making process?

PROSPECT: Well [eyes level and to his left], the agent *told* us that the school in the area was real good and that was important to us, of course, having three kids [auditory recalled externally].

MP: What was the next thing that helped you make your decision to buy the home?

PROSPECT: [Eyes up and to the left.] I guess when we *saw* that the inside was just as nice looking as the outside, we just [eyes level and to the left] told each other, "Let's go for it," and we did [visual external, then auditory external].

You could go on, but really, you have what you need.

$$Vr + K + Ar + Vr + Ar \longrightarrow decision$$

Strategy Elicitation

We have a general strategy for most anything we do in life. We drive to work in a similar manner each day. This habitual pattern is laid down in the brain so that we don't even have to consciously think about where we are going. We get in the car, turn it on, and end up at work. This pattern is made up of many small elements that, when combined and consciously considered, make up a strategy for getting to work.

In order to learn someone's strategy for getting to work, falling in love, buying a product, or anything else, we must ask questions. The following questions allow us to elicit someone's strategy from them.

1. "Can you remember a time when you were completely X [for example, happy with the purchase of your house, happy you went out with someone new, in love, etc.]?"

2. "Can you remember, fully, a specific time?"

3. "What was the very first thing that caused you to be X?"
    a. "Was it something you saw?"
    b. "Was it something you heard?"
    c. "Was it something you felt?"
    d. "What was the very first thing that caused you to be *completely* X?"

4. "What was the very next thing that caused you to be X?"
    a. "Was it something you saw?"
    b. "Was it something you heard?"
    c. "Was it something you felt inside?"
    d. "What was it?"

5. "Were you completely X at this point?"
    a. If yes, elicitation is complete.
    b. If no, continue with number 4.

Obviously, we will not be able to use these exact words in all persuasive settings. So, you will have to adjust your questions to gain information in each different context.

Elicit the strategies for love, happiness, and decision making from people you know. Do this with at least three people. As you do so, write out precisely what the person's strategy for that result or process is. Use the questions you learned above. If you have a hard time with them, don't worry about it. The point of the questions is to remind you that there are specific stages in each person's strategies. The key point to always remember is that it's not just a picture or sound that makes someone want something or someone. There are a number of components and thought processes involved. After you have finished this exercise, continue with the ones below, which as you remember are critical to complete!

Exercises

1. Focus a video camera on yourself from the vantage point of your listener sitting at a table. Sell your product to the camera if you are alone. Better: Sell your product to a friend with a presentation you have written based upon the knowledge you've gained from this book. Build rapport, identify needs, discover values, give your presentation, handle resistance, confirm the sale.

2. Focus the camera on your counterpart as you give another proposal to him.

3. Watch the presentations back to back. Both of you should comment extensively on the following. When viewing Exercise 1, were you congruent? Did your voice match your

words, or did you send mixed messages? Watch your eye movements. When you notice eye movement, how does it relate to your terminology as far as visual, auditory, and kinesthetic words are concerned? Are you using words that represent your representations, or do you "translate" to fit *your* counterpart's?

4. As you view Exercise 2, you and your friend are to consider how your friend responded to you. Does your friend appear defensive, or in rapport? Why? What do his eye movements reveal? Are there times when something you say or do affect your friend in a way that surprises you? How so?

5. After viewing the videos, ask your friend to comment on what he saw, what he heard, and how he felt through each segment of your meeting.

6. After gaining this feedback from both viewing the videotape and hearing the insights of your friend, what can you do to improve your skills in the persuasion process?

7. Videotape should be used constantly to give you feedback on your progress at becoming a Master Persuader. At least once each month you should tape one to two hours of video. The more vantage points you can get, the better.

8. Each month when you do your videotaping, you should choose a controversial subject like abortion, religion, politics, foreign affairs, or war and for ten to twenty minutes attempt to persuade your friend to the side you strongly *disagree* with. Your friend should defend your normal belief or point of view.

At this point you have the opportunity to master part 2 of this book. We have now reached the end, of the beginning. Begin to change the direction of your life today so that your dreams may all come true!

Ethics

The WIN/WIN philosophy promoted in this book is an ideal. As an ideal it is something that is never in perfect balance. Ethics is generally defined as a system of moral principles. The statement itself begs the question, "Whose principles?"

A religious person would answer, "God's principles."

The return question is then, "Whose definition of God's principles?"

If I'm an Orthodox Jew, my principles differ from most Christians'. I won't eat pork at any price. I rest on Sabbath without exception. If I'm a Southern Baptist Christian, I won't play cards or dance but I'll eat pork and go to church on Sunday instead of Sabbath. If I'm a Catholic, I will play cards and dance but I won't eat fish on Friday and I will give up something for Lent every year.

Religious beliefs are the basis of many of our principles of behavior. We think that people who don't adhere to our beliefs and principles are essentially inferior to us. It is for just this reason that the subject of ethics is presented in this way for you to consider. The author of this book has no more right to tell you what is right or wrong than does your neighbor. Most of our culture agrees certain things are bad (murder, rape, child abuse . . .) and certain things are good (volunteerism, charity, friendliness . . .). But what about all the behaviors and social interactions in between?

If you go to a car dealership and pay invoice price on a car, is that a WIN/WIN deal or does it seem as if you are getting the better deal? What if I tell you that the dealer is getting a factory-to-dealer rebate of $1,500? The dealer could have passed on half of the rebate to you and still profited $750 plus end-of-year incentives on the car. Now you know the dealer is getting the rebate. Did you get taken advantage of? At what point does the scale balance? It is different for each person of course.

Imagine that you are the spouse of a paraplegic who has no insurance to cover his medical expenses and you have no money for food. Your children are literally starving and you have no money, no credit, and no one to borrow money from. Every cent that you can earn or beg is going to your spouse's needs. Is it ethical to steal food for your children? Is it ethical *not* to provide food for your children? If you say that you should never take what is not yours, then you are faced with the death of your children. How do you explain this to your children? Ethics is clearly a very personal matter. What is more important, principles or life?

Would you ever hit your spouse? What if someone gave you $1,000? What if someone gave you $100,000 to hit your spouse, just one time? How about $1,000,000? What if your spouse said it was all right, then would it be OK? Is there ever a point when striking someone is ethical?

At what point do we determine that we will no longer pay our taxes? As of this writing, taxes eat up about a quarter of our income. Will we refuse to pay taxes when the government takes half of our money? What if it took 75 percent of our money? What if it took it all and then decided how we would live and where? Is it ever ethical to disobey your country? How do you know? Where is the *exact* line?

On the face of it, ethics seem pretty simple. Don't cheat any-one and don't get cheated. Unfortunately, everyone operates out of his own reality. Honest people can belong to both the Democratic and Republican parties. How do we know which is best? At what point do we call someone a "cultist" for the religion he belongs to? Is every religion a cult? Are no religions cults? Where is the precise line of division? Many honest and sincere people belong to what most Americans call cults or fringe political groups. At what point is it ethical to be prejudiced against people who are different than we are?

Each of us has his own answers to these questions. Some of the above questions we may struggle with. In the end, we will decide that our morals are superior to those of others. It is my hope that while you will believe that your ethics are of the highest standard, you also consider that there are other systems of morals. The people who adhere to these other systems are just as sincere as you are.

Now, decide at what point the dealer and the car buyer have an exact WIN/WIN scenario.

APPENDIX B

Brainwashing

Each day the average American is bombarded with thousands of messages from various media sources that shape the way we think. Unless you are completely aware of the *purpose* behind the billboards and print and television advertising, you will quickly become part of the "mainstream."

The last thing any politician wants is for you to have a *variety* of behaviors or choice in your life. Why? The more variety you have, the more complicated it becomes to predict your behavior. The more difficult it is to predict your behavior, the less chance the politician has to persuade you. The politician wants you predictable. When people become predictable, those who understand the persuasion process will apply it with ease to reach their objectives. Unfortunately, many people who understand the persuasion process are not looking for WIN/WIN scenarios.

When a group of people wants you to change your way of thinking to its way of thinking without consideration of your values or beliefs, this is brainwashing. In the author's opinion, brainwashing as defined here is unethical in most cases, but not all. As with "ethics," "brainwashing" must be evaluated within the context of each individual's values. Therefore, my

271

opinions about brainwashing are not as important as yours. What follows is the general methodology used to reorient, indoctrinate, and/or brainwash people in groups.

How do governments, groups, religions, and political organizations implement mind control? The author appreciates the Christian religion and the United States military as great institutions. Therefore we will consider examples of reorientation from these areas. I wish to assure you that I am not knocking any religion! Any belief needs to be respected or communication is not possible.

1. Effective mind control is very difficult to accomplish without moving individuals away from or completely out of their current environment. When you enlist in the military you enter what is called "basic training" or "boot camp." This is the first step toward reorienting the enlistee's mind. A new set of values will be instilled shortly, but the essential element here is the elimination of the old enviroment and the installation of the individual into the new environment. The old pattern of the young person going home at the end of a day of work is quickly eliminated. The new environment is normally communal in nature. In order for the new values to be instilled in the recruits, it must be!

If the recruit could go home at the end of every day of BT and was allowed to discuss the daily events with family and friends, value indoctrination, which follows, could take forever. The only people the military wants you to talk with are people in the military. After basic training, the recruit will be transferred *far* from home and far from anywhere he has affiliation with. This will assure the "military as home" imprinting.

If a recruit cannot succeed in the new environment, which is rare but does happen, he/she will be discharged at this point. An individual who refuses to work within his new environment will not make a good soldier, will not follow orders, and will not align his values with those of his unit and the military hierarchy. This person is a detriment to the military. (We will follow the recruit throughout the process but will add another example here for a deeper understanding of brainwashing.)

Meanwhile, there is another individual who has become unhappy with his church or religion and wants to begin his search for truth. Generally when people begin to search, they go to groups of people, in this case, churches or other religous organizations.

Once a person has walked in the door and has experienced displeasure with his past affiliation and desire for a new affiliation, he can be manipulated. In most cases of reorientation (brainwashing), the individual will be asked to come to the church as much as possible to learn the beliefs of the organization. (indoctrination). This is necessary for the new "recruit" to function within the group environment. Every church, cult, or group has its own language. People from other groups often have no idea what the words and concepts of another group mean. (For example, if you are not Catholic, can you explain "purgatory" and be certain of its meaning? If you are not a Baptist or in a related group, can you fully explain "rapture" with certainty of its meaning? If you are not a Mormon can you with certainty explain "celestial Heaven"? If you are not in an Eastern religion like Buddhism or Hinduism, can you with certainty explain "dharma"? In general, most people do not understand the language of other groups. This is the second part of reorientation and indoctrination.)

2. Learning the language is the next binding element between the recruit and the group. Returning to our young person in boot camp, not only is he learning to accept his new conditions (being awakened at the same time every day, with the same routine, same lunchtime, same dinnertime, same bedtime, etc.), he is learning the new language of the people he will be working with. In the military, the new language consists of the terminology of rank, new words for old jobs (cooking

dinner for the troops is "KP"), new words for new jobs, abbre-
viations, and so on. It is a complete transformation. It is very
necessary. When the recruit discusses his new environment
with his old friends, they feel distanced from him. They no
longer understand him as they used to. He is beginning to
change. He is different.

Back at the other group or church the individual is learning
the language of the group. The more time he spends with the
group, the faster he learns the language. The faster he learns
the language, the quicker he gains rapport with those in the
group. As he gains rapport with the group, the people begin
to like him and he likes them. Conversely, the people outside
the group do not speak the same language and therefore are
not as interesting to the recruit as his newfound friends. The
people outside feel that the recruit is beginning to change.
They begin to feel uncomfortable around their old friend. He
is different.

3. Deprogramming old beliefs and values is the next logical
step for any group to take with its new members. It is very subtle, but very important to the next level. Here's what happens.

In the military, where threat of physical and emotional punishment can be carried out, deprogramming occurs quickly.
The drill sergeant becomes the dominant parental figure to
each new recruit. The old mother is at home. The sergeant is
the new mother, like it or not. He will make decisions arbi-
trarily if he chooses, and will expect complete obedience to
every order. With the deprogramming of the belief that you
can select your own wake-up time, bedtime, lunchtime, and all
other past ritualistic behavior, the ground is laid for new programming to be imprinted. Because the military has the
threat of punishment and the person cannot refuse obedience, he must agree to be deprogrammed. No longer are his
old friends his true friends. He's here; they're there. They
won't ever be here for the recruit.

In another group environment like a church or cult, the

threat of physical punishment is normally low, with a few exceptions, and the threat of emotional punishment is high in almost all cases.

Our friend who became part of the religous group has now learned the language and is being slowly deprogrammed. When the person walked in the door, there was no commitment necessary of any major significance. The person was there to learn. As the person learns the "truth" he is gently shown how his old friends and family were mistaken. He is shown how they are missing out. The person is shown how some of his old beliefs and values simply don't mesh with the "truth." The newcomer is usually asked to point out that he sees where he was wrong or previously misled. He is asked to agree that his previous belief structure was flawed. This can be done with great subtlety. The important point is that he was wrong and has now discovered the "truth." The final and very important part of deprogramming is deprogramming the perceived value of relationships outside the religious group. The person is normally not asked to give up all contact forever, but is made to understand that to dwell with "evil" or those who practice "evil" is dangerous and therefore communication with people on the outside must be done with great care.

4. Reprogramming the individual with new beliefs and values where the voids have been created is the next step.

We all have some very basic needs. We all need food, clothing, and shelter. We need to feel secure. We each need to have a "mother figure" in our life, real or imagined (someone who takes care of us whom we bond to regardless of whether or not we like the person at all times). Once a void is created in the individual by being away from his mother, spouse, loved ones, and/or friends, the void will be filled by the new group's leader and the individual's closest affiliates in the new group. This often occurs as early as stage one.

Old beliefs are now replaced with new beliefs. Old authority figures are now replaced with new authority figures. "Truth" replaces "fiction." "Good behavior" is rewarded in order to condition the new member toward obedience.

The young man in the military will imprint on his sergeant as his mother figure. He will learn that his fellow recruits are the people that will save his life when the chips are down. The family and friends will be at home in a warm beds while they are lying out in foxholes in the desert. The unit that he is part of has now replaced his family as his family. The corps has replaced other organizational affiliations. The young man's best friend is now one of his fellow recruits. It *must* be this way for the safety of all concerned. Unfortunately, when someone leaves the service, the belief structure generally remains intact. Fitting back into society is very difficult for many and therefore they will stay in the military as long as possible. The various military codes replace all previous doctrines of high value.

Meanwhile, back at the religious group, the individual is spending more time with the flock. The reprogramming replaces old values and beliefs with the "truth." To ever leave the truth and return to the old ways would mean the greatest of punishment. The person is taught that once one has found the truth, to turn one's back on it would be unforgivable. The person agrees completely. Generally at the early stages there is no need for the negative reinforcement. The "truth" is still in the discovery stage and not the "uncovering" stage. The values and beliefs become rearranged and once they are set in place it will be very difficult ever to change them again.

5. Finally, disciples become teachers. When the individual is fully reoriented and indoctrinated, he is ready to spread the good news. When communicating with people on the outside he will be surprised that everyone doesn't see as clearly as he does now. In the military, some of these people will become recruiters. Most will not participate in recruiting as their full-time military job, however. The individual simply through conversation passes on his obvious governmental benefits, which are great and many to be sure. He tells his "old" friends of the security he has. In the religious groups, some of these people

will become evangelists for their group. It is well known that the best way to learn something is to teach it. It is also well known through the law of consistency that once you teach something to someone or tell something to someone it is very hard to admit later that you were incorrect in any respect. Once a person enters stage five, turning back is a rare occurrence.

It is here that the cycle of brainwashing is essentially complete. The process is reinforced daily and is perceived as more real and clear as each day passes. With the individual spending a maximum amount of time with the new group, whatever it is, he will run into very little "outside" resistance. The less resistance the person runs into, the more likely his new beliefs will be validated over and over again.

The military is not really a "brainwashing" group, is it? Or does it have to be, out of necessity for the security of its people? If it were a brainwashing group for the common good, would it then be acceptable? I cannot answer that question. Each person who enters the military today does so willingly. The same can be said for most political, religious, and philosophical organizations. Therefore the answers lie within you. The answers lie within the moral systems that are within you.

Many people have decided that cults brainwash people. Look at the following list of Christian religions. Place a check mark by the cults.

Catholic	Jehovah's Witnesses
Lutheran	Seventh-Day Adventist
Pentecostal	Christian Scientist
Methodist	

As you made your decisions, what specific criteria did you use? Do any of the religions that you did *not* check use brainwashing techniques as noted above?

Each day as you consider schools, churches, civic groups,

fraternal organizations, corporations, governments, and all other groups, you will notice something interesting. They *all* use brainwashing to some degree. Is this good or bad? Why? How could a better system be set in place?

Glossary

Belief—Generalization, often of great importance to an individual. Often relates to cause and effect and our behaviors, capabilities, and identities. Difficult to alter with logical reasoning or argumentation. Emotional in nature and strongly linked to values.

Congruent—When a person's beliefs, strategies, and behaviors are all in alignment. This means that others receive similar verbal and nonverbal messages.

Elicitation—The designed uncovering of specific strategies and other processes in an individual.

Future pacing—Preparing ahead of time the outcome of some belief, behavior, or strategy.

Hypnosis—The art and science of altering the perceptions, processes, and states of mind of the self or others.

Kinesthetic—Relating to sensations or emotions.

Master Persuader—Any person who is unconsciously competent in the use of persuasion and communication strategies, techniques, and skills.

Meta Program—A content-free program that is a deep filter for communication and behavior. The same Meta Program is often context related. (For example, a person may move "toward" pleasure in personal relationships while also moving "away" from pain in business.)

Neuro-Linguistic Programming—The science and art of modeling other people in order to produce similar behaviors and results in the self or other people. The term was coined in 1975 by Richard Bandler while studying with his partner, John Grinder. These two gentlemen modeled the most effective therapists in the world (Milton H. Erickson, Gregory Bateson, Fritz Perls, Virginia Satir, etc.).

Proxemics—The study of human use of physical space; how people behave relative to spatial conditions.

Rapport—Relation characterized by harmony, accord, or affinity.

Reframing—Changing the context of a situation; putting a "new frame" on an old picture; looking at the same thing from a different point of view.

Skill—Any learned ability.

State—The combination of a person's immediate thoughts and physiology at any given moment.

Strategy—A specific set of steps, both internal and external, that a person or group must take to reach an objective.

Values—What we try to obtain or attain in our life. (We try to obtain means values and attain ends values.) Values also include those things we move away from most strongly.

Bibliography

Allesandra, Tony. *Non-Manipulative Selling.* New York: Simon and Schuster, 1987.

Andreas, Steve and Connirae. *Change Your Mind.* Moab, Utah: Real People Press, 1987.

Bagley, Dan. *Beyond Selling.* Cupertino, Calif.: Meta Publications, 1987.

Bandler, Richard. *Frogs into Princes: Neuro Linguistic Programming.* Moab, Utah: Real People Press, 1979.

Birdwhistell, Ray L. *Kinesics and Context: Essays on Body Motion Communication.* Philadelphia: University of Pennsylvania Press, 1970.

Blanchard, Kenneth H. *One Minute Manager Meets the Monkey.* New York: William Morrow, 1989.

Brislin, Richard. *Understanding Culture's Influence of Behavior.* New York: Harcourt Brace Jovanovich, 1993.

Britannica. *Encyclopedia Britannica.* New York: 1991.

283

Carnegie, Dale. *How to Win Friends and Influence People*. 1936. Reprint. New York: Pocket Books, 1990.

Chu, Chin-ning. *Asian Mind Game: Unlocking the Hidden Agenda of the Asian Business Culture*. New York: Macmillan, 1991.

———. *Thick Face, Black Heart: Thriving, Winning and Succeeding in Life's Every Endeavor*. Antioch, Calif.: AMC Publishing, 1992.

Cialdini, Robert B. *Influence: The New Psychology of Modern Persuasion*. New York: William Morrow, 1985.

Cohen, Herb. *Art of Negotiation*. New York: Bantam, 1980.

Dawson, Roger. *You Can Get Anything You Want: But You Have to Do More Than Ask*. New York: Simon and Schuster, 1985.

Dilts, Robert. *Applications of NLP: '78-'84*. Cupertino, Calif.: Meta Publications, 1983.

———. *Changing Belief Systems with NLP*. Cupertino, Calif.: Meta Publications, 1993.

Drozdeck, Steven. *What They Don't Teach You in Sales 101*. New York: McGraw-Hill, 1991.

Dyer, Wayne W. *Your Erroneous Zones*. 1976. Reprint. New York: HarperCollins, 1993.

Edwards, Douglas. *Sales Closing Power*. Placerville, Calif.: Hampton House Publishing, 1984.

Grinder, John. *The Structure of Magic, Vol. 1*. Palo Alto, Calif.: Science and Behavior Books, 1976.

Gschwandtner, Gerhard and Patricia Garnett. *How to Become a Master Sales Builder: Personal Selling Power's Blueprint for Success.* Englewood Cliffs, N.J.: Prentice Hall, 1987.

Hall, Edward T. *The Silent Language.* 1959. Reprint. New York: Doubleday, 1973.

———. *The Hidden Dimension.* 1966. Reprint. New York: Doubleday, 1990.

Hill, Napoleon. *Law of Success.* Evanston, Ill.: Success Unlimited, 1977.

Hoffer, Eric. *The True Believer: Thoughts on the Nature of Mass Movements.* 1951. Reprint. New York: HarperCollins, 1989.

Hogan, Kevin L. *Building Positive Kids.* St. Paul, Minn.: Success Dynamics, 1989.

———. *The Gift: A Discovery of Happiness, Fulfillment, and Love.* Eagan, Minn.: Network 3000, 1992.

Holy Bible, King James Version.

Hopkins, Tom. *How to Master the Art of Selling.* New York: Warner Books. 1988.

James, Tad. *Time Line Therapy.* Cupertino, Calif.: Meta Publications, 1988.

Jung, Carl. *Psychological Types.* New York: Harcourt, Brace, 1923.

Kiersey, David. *Please Understand Me.* Del Mar, Calif.: Prometheus Nemesis Book Co., 1978.

Knapp, Mark and Judy Hall. *Nonverbal Communication in Human Interaction*. 3d ed. Fort Worth: Harcourt Brace College Publications, 1992.

Kostere, Kim. *Get the Results You Want: A Systematic Approach to NLP.* Portland, Oreg.: Metamorphous Press, 1989.

Lewis, David. *The Secret Language of Success: Using Body Language to Get What You Want*. New York: Carroll & Graf, 1990.

McGinnis, Alan L. *Bringing Out the Best in People: How to Enjoy Helping Others Excel.* Minneapolis: Augsburg Fortress, 1985.

Maltz, Maxwell. *Psycho-Cybernetics*. North Hollywood, Calif.: Wilshire Book Co., 1973.

Maslow, Abraham. *Motivation and Personality*. New York: Harper, 1954.

Mehrabian, Albert. *Silent Messages: Implicit Communication of Emotions and Attitudes*. Belmont, Calif.: Wadsworth, 1981.

Molloy, John. *Molloy's Live for Success*. New York: Bantam, 1985.

Ogilvy, David. *Ogilvy on Advertising*. New York: Random House, 1985.

Overstreet, H. A. *Influencing Human Behavior.* New York: Norton, 1925.

Pratkanis, Anthony. *Age of Propaganda*. New York: W. H. Freeman, 1991.

Richardson, Jerry. *The Magic of Rapport*. Cupertino, Calif.: Meta Publications, 1988.

Ringer, Robert J. *Million Dollar Habits*. Grand Rapids, Mich.: Revell, 1990.

Robbins, Anthony. *Unlimited Power*. New York: Fawcett, 1987.

Sommer, R. *Personal Space*. Englewood Cliffs, N.J.: Prentice Hall, 1969.

Tracy, Brian. *Psychology of Selling*. Chicago: Nightingale Conant, 1988. Sound cassette.

Vitale, Joe. *The Seven Lost Secrets of Success*. Houston: VistaTron, 1994.

Waitley, Denis. *The Psychology of Winning*. New York: Berkley, 1984.

Wilson, Robert A. *Prometheus Rising*. Santa Monica, Calif.: New Falcon, 1993.

———. *Quantum Psychology*. Santa Monica, Calif.: New Falcon, 1993.

Ziglar, Zig. *Goals*. Chicago: Nightingale Conant, 1988. Sound cassette.

———. *See You at the Top*. Gretna, La.: Pelican, 1984.

———. *Steps to the Top*. Gretna, La.: Pelican, 1985.

———. *Ziglar on Selling: The Ultimate Handbook of the Complete Sales Professional*. New York: Ballantine, 1993.